RED

GREG LAURIE

RED

THE COLOR OF CHRISTMAS

15 FAVORITE CHRISTMAS MESSAGES

ALLEN DAVID BOOKS

Red: The Color of Christmas, 15 Favorite Christmas Messages

Art direction: Greg Laurie
Art production: Mark Ferjulian
Cover design: Michael Berger
Copy Editor: Karla Pedrow

ISBN 978-1-942090-05-2

Cataloging-in-Publication Data is available.

Printed in the United States of America

1 2 3 4 5 6 7 8 / 19 18 17 16 15 14

CONTENTS

INTRODUCTION

THE COLOR OF CHRISTMAS

We have all wondered, from time to time, whether we might have missed the real meaning of Christmas.

People say, "It's too commercial" or maybe, "It's too materialistic." Others of us say, "It's become too politically correct."

But here is one thing we might not have considered: *we may have made it too beautiful.*

Most of us, whether we grew up in a Christian home or not, can call to mind Christmas card images of snowy countrysides, horse-drawn sleighs, wreaths of holly, frosty windows, red candles, rosy-cheeked carolers clad in scarves and hats, and softly glowing colored lights. Besides these, we have all the lovely biblical images as well: mother and child, animals in the stable, adoring shepherds, and richly robed wise men following a wondrous star across the heavens. It's all so beautiful. And in many ways, the first Christmas *was* beautiful.

But here's what we might forget: the beautiful baby born in the manger in Bethlehem came with a distinct purpose. That mission was to grow up, and in the very prime of His life, surrender Himself to the horrors of a Roman cross, shed His blood, and die for the sins of the world.

Yes, there is much wonder and beauty in what God accomplished on that Christmas two-thousand-plus years ago, and we're right to be in awe of it. But all of Heaven knew the real reason why Jesus came to Earth and was born as a human baby. It wasn't just to teach everyone to be good and love his or her neighbor; it was to die an agonizing death to ransom us from an eternal death sentence.

He came as a Redeemer. The shadow of the cross lay over the beauty of that first Christmas night.

Think of Mary, proudly carrying her newborn son into the temple to have Him circumcised according to the Law. An old man named Simeon took the Child in his arms and prophesied over Him, speaking of light and salvation and glory. But before he turned away, he had a sober message for Mary: "Yes, a sword will pierce through your own soul also" (Luke 2:35).

Within the joy, within the wonder, there is also pain . . . and the red blood paid to redeem us.

At Christmas we decorate our trees with festive lights and ornaments. But the real "tree" in the Christmas story wasn't beautiful at all; it was a cruel instrument of execution, used to bring about the death of God's Son. The Bible says, "Cursed is everyone who hangs on a tree" (Galatians 3:13). Jesus hung on that tree and became sin for us (see 2 Corinthians 5:21). He was born to die so that we might live.

RED

Isaiah 1:18 says, " 'Come now, and let us reason together,' says the LORD, 'Though your sins are like scarlet, they shall be as white as snow; though they are red like crimson, they shall be as wool.' "

Red is the color of Christmas. It is not because Santa wore red or because we wrap our presents in red paper or attach red bows on top of holly wreaths or put red bulbs and lights on our trees. Red is the color of Christmas for a different reason altogether and doesn't fit in with the way our culture celebrates December 25. The Christmas color of red isn't random; it is the color of the blood that flowed from the wounds of Jesus Christ as He died for the sins of the world, making available to you the greatest gift you could ever receive in a billion times a billion years.

The apostle Paul said, "Thank God for this gift, his gift. No language can praise it enough!" (2 Corinthians 9:15, MSG). This is truly the only gift that literally keeps on giving: the gift of eternal life through Jesus Christ our Lord. C. S. Lewis put it best when he said the Son of God became a man that men might become sons of God.

Jesus was born, lived, died, and rose again from the dead so that you could come into a relationship with God, receive the gift of eternal life, and live life with meaning and purpose.

That is the real message of Christmas. Let every glimpse of red remind you of the greatest gift of all.

PART ONE

CHRISTMAS, BC

1

BEFORE BETHLEHEM

Though I have seated myself in front of the computer to write about Christmas joy, I have to be honest here. Shopping can *really* stress me out in December. This year especially, it seems like everything ended up costing a whole lot more than I thought it would.

It reminds me of "The Twelve Days of Christmas." You know that tune, don't you? It's kind of a bizarre song when you think about it. I suppose it's speaking about the extravagance of buying just the right presents for your true love. But when you total the price of all those presents over the twelve days, you'd have to be Bill Gates or Donald Trump to pull it all off.

It starts, of course, with a partridge in a pear tree. (Something that's never been particularly high on my Christmas list.) Then there are two turtle doves, three French hens, four calling birds, five golden rings, six geese a-laying, seven swans a-swimming, and on it goes. Experts put the cost of all 364 items mentioned in the song at $65,264.

By the way, that's up 19 percent from a year ago.

Eight maids a-milking and ten lords a-leaping are about the same price as last year, but the eleven pipers and twelve drummers must belong to a musicians' union, because they are 28 percent more expensive than last season.

I don't know about you, but I'm ready to be done with it—not with the celebration of the birth of Jesus, of course, but with all the hoopla of Christmas. Most of us aren't really sick of Christmas; we're sick of what it has become in our culture. But when we set all the accouterments and add-ons aside and just get back into the simple account of our Lord's birth in the Scriptures, joy springs up like an artesian well.

And that's exactly what we need to get back to.

As I see it, here's our main problem: many of us try to find joy and happiness in Christmas when we really need to find joy and happiness in Christ Himself. And that is a very big difference.

When you place your hopes and expectations on a particular celebration or a special day on the calendar, you'll find yourself disappointed again and again. But when you place your hopes and expectations on the Lord Himself, He will never, never let you down.

> And this hope will not lead to disappointment. For we know how dearly God loves us, because he has given us the Holy Spirit to fill our hearts with his love. (Romans 5:5, NLT)

BEFORE BETHLEHEM

I love the Christmas story and never get tired of hearing it or telling it. It truly is the most powerful of all stories. And best of all, it's completely true!

But the real story of Christmas goes way, way back before Bethlehem, before Mary and Joseph, before the shepherds and wise men and innkeepers and King Herod and all of the people who played a part at that great hinge of history two thousand years ago. In fact, the first mention of Christmas was BC.

BC? How could that be? Doesn't BC stand for "Before Christ"? How could there be a Christmas story before Jesus came?

The answer is simply this: The story of Christmas is actually an integral part of an even greater story that goes all the way back to the beginning. It is the story of our redemption.

Interestingly enough, the account in the Scriptures begins with a tree—not a Christmas tree but "the tree of the knowledge of good and evil." God Himself placed that tree in the midst of the Garden of Eden, the incredible paradise where our first parents, Adam and Eve, lived.

Those first two human beings experienced radiant beauty at every turn of those garden paths, with stunning trees, soft breezes, and magnificent flowers—most likely beyond what we have ever seen or even imagined. They also had exotic wildlife and the companionship of the animal kingdom, with creatures that would never and could never hurt them. Best of all by far, they enjoyed unbroken daily fellowship with their Creator. The world at that time was completely free of sin and all the guilt, shame, grief, and dark shadows that accompany it.

And what was Adam and Eve's assignment? Basically, they were to discover, oversee, and enjoy all that God had placed in that lovely heaven on earth.

But there was one prohibition. Just one:

> But the LORD God warned him, "You may freely eat the fruit of every tree in the garden—except the tree of the knowledge of good and evil. If you eat its fruit, you are sure to die." (Genesis 2:16–17, NLT)

Most of us have heard how Adam and Eve stood by that tree and listened to the voice of the Tempter, who suggested they would do well to disobey God and eat of the fruit that He had restricted. He hissed, "You won't die! . . . God knows that your eyes will be opened as soon as you eat it, and you will be like God, knowing both good and evil" (Genesis 3:4–5, NLT).

The tragic record goes on to state:

> The woman was convinced. She saw that the tree was beautiful and its fruit looked delicious, and she wanted

the wisdom it would give her. So she took some of the fruit and ate it. Then she gave some to her husband, who was with her, and he ate it, too. At that moment their eyes were opened, and they suddenly felt shame at their nakedness. So they sewed fig leaves together to cover themselves. (verses 6–7, NLT)

Their eyes were opened, all right; Satan was right about that part. But they did not become just like God. In fact, they lost the most precious possession in their lives, far more important than their beautiful Eden, or even each other. They lost their relationship and that sweet fellowship with their Creator.

When the cool evening breezes were blowing, the man and his wife heard the LORD God walking about in the garden. So they hid from the LORD God among the trees. Then the LORD God called to the man, "Where are you?"

He replied, "I heard you walking in the garden, so I hid. I was afraid because I was naked."

"Who told you that you were naked?" the LORD God asked. "Have you eaten from the tree whose fruit I commanded you not to eat?" (verses 8–11, NLT)

What followed was the first miserable excuse in all of human history. And wouldn't you know it, it began with a man complaining about his wife and basically was followed with "the Devil made me do it."

> The man replied, "It was the woman you gave me who gave me the fruit, and I ate it."
>
> Then the LORD God asked the woman, "What have you done?"
>
> "The serpent deceived me," she replied. "That's why I ate it." (verses 12–13, NLT)

What follows is the first Christmas verse in the Bible. No, it's not Isaiah 9:6, that well-loved passage that prophesies the coming of Jesus as Wonderful, Counselor, Mighty God, Everlasting Father, and Prince of Peace. Nor is it Micah 5:2 that speaks of little Bethlehem among the thousands of Judah.

The fact is, you may have never heard of Genesis 3:15 referred to as a Christmas passage, but that is just what it is. Why? Because it's the very first verse in the Bible that speaks of the Coming One who would accomplish our salvation.

It is the first *red* verse in the Scriptures.

The words come from God Himself and are directed at Satan:

And I will put enmity
Between you and the woman,

And between your seed and her Seed;

He shall bruise your head,

And you shall bruise His heel.

By these words God was drawing the battle lines and saying, "Game on." The Lord was telling the Devil that the Coming One would crush his head. Yes, the Evil One would bruise His heel, but in the process, the Redeemer would smash the head of Satan.

From that time forward, then, Satan has been watching and waiting for this expected Deliverer: the Christ, the Messiah. And knowing as he did that this Savior would come through the Jewish people, he did everything in his power to stop the birth of the Promised One before it could happen. You can trace it right through the Old Testament. In the book of Exodus, you can find Pharaoh, king of Egypt, systematically executing all the newborn baby boys. But ultimately, the Lord raised up Moses to go back to Egypt and lead His people out of that land in a great exodus.

Then you fast-forward to the book of Esther, and you see the plot of the wicked man known as Haman, who wanted to execute all of the Jews. It's so easy to see the hand of Satan in this. Haman began with wanted revenge on one lone Jew, Mordecai, but he became swallowed up by rage that knew no bounds. He tried to kill every Jew in the world.

Over in the New Testament, in the gospel of Matthew, we have the plot of King Herod to kill all the baby boys, two years old and under, in the region of Bethlehem. He'd gotten word from the traveling Magi about a coming King who would be born in that town, and inspired by Satan, he tried to kill the Messiah by slaughtering all the baby boys in the vicinity.

As bloody and horrific as these attempts must have been, no one and nothing could stop the Messiah from being born because God always keeps His appointments. And at the right moment, the Lord came to us, born in that manger in Bethlehem. As it says in the book of Galatians, "But when the fullness of the time had come, God sent forth His Son, born of a woman" (4:4).

But was that where Jesus began?

JESUS IN THE BEFORE DAYS

Did Jesus preexist before Bethlehem? Was there a Jesus before the Nativity?

The answer is yes.

Bethlehem was the time and location where the Incarnation took place, that is, when God became a man. But that is *not* when Jesus came into being. Jesus is God, and as God, He is eternal; He always has been and always will be. In the book of Revelation, He says, "I am the First and the Last. I am the Living One; I was dead, and now look, I am alive for ever and ever!" (1:17–18, NIV).

Even though both Matthew and Luke chose to begin their gospels with the birth of Christ, John's gospel begins by going back before, before, before, to the very beginning of everything:

> In the beginning was the Word, and the Word was with God, and the Word was God. He was in the beginning with God. All things were made through Him, and without Him nothing was made that was made. In Him was life, and the life was the light of men. And the light shines in the darkness, and the darkness did not comprehend it. (1:1–5)

Most of our Bible translations have a definite article before the word *beginning*. We read, "In the beginning was *the* Word" (emphasis added). In the original language, however, there is no definite article. That means you cannot pinpoint the moment in time where there was a beginning, because John is looking all the way back through time to eternity past. He is going back farther than our minds can imagine.

Jesus existed before there was a world, before there were planets, stars, and galaxies, before there was light and darkness, before there was any matter whatsoever. The Godhead is eternal. Jesus

Christ is coequal, coeternal, and coexistent with the Father and the Holy Spirit. He was with God. He was God. He *is* God.

When Jesus entered our world as a human being, He became an embryo and then . . . a Deity in diapers. Jesus left the safety of Heaven, stepped into time and space, breathed our air, shared our pain, walked in our shoes, lived our life, and died our death.

Jesus did not become identical to us, but He did become identified with us. In fact, He could not have identified with us any more closely than He did. It was total identification without the loss of identity, because He became one of us without ceasing to be Himself. He became human without ceasing to be God.

It sort of blows the mind to think about, but Jesus Christ was fully God *and* fully man. Now when I say "fully man," I don't mean that He had the capacity to sin. Being God, that could not or would not happen. Yet He was a man in a human body, feeling human emotion, facing physical limitations, and experiencing real pain. Though actual blood coursed through His veins, He was and is Deity, God in human form.

The Christmas carol says it well:

Veiled in flesh, the Godhead see,
Hail th' incarnate Deity!
Pleased as man with men to dwell,
Jesus, our Emmanuel.

John, chapter 1, tells us that "the Word was with God" (verse 1). This literally means that "the word was *continually toward* God." This gives us a glimpse into the relationship of Father, Son, and Holy Spirit. The preposition *with* carries the idea of nearness, along with a sense of movement, toward God. That's another way of saying there always has been the deepest equality and intimacy within the Trinity. Jesus summed it up in John 17 when He prayed to the Father, "And now, O Father, glorify Me together with Yourself, with the glory which I had with You before the world was" (verse 5).

One popular paraphrase translates the verse like this:

And now, Father, glorify me with your very own splendor, the very splendor I had in your presence before there was a world. (MSG)

Before there was a world! There was never a time when Christ did not exist. Yet this eternal Son of God became a man, and that is what we celebrate at Christmas. In Isaiah 9:6, written centuries before the Lord's birth in Bethlehem, the prophet said of Him, "For unto us a Child is born, unto us *a Son is given*" (emphasis added). This passage perfectly sums up what happened on Christmas, giving us both the heavenly and earthly perspectives. We tend to view Christmas from our viewpoint: the Child being born. But then Isaiah gives it from the heavenly perspective: *a Son is given*. Christmas, then, is the story of an arrival, but it is also the story of a departure. He arrived on Earth, but He departed from Heaven.

BC APPEARANCES OF JESUS

The theologians have a word for it: *theophany*. What it means is an appearance of God. We might also use the word *Christophany*, which means an appearance of Christ before Bethlehem. Are all theophanies Christophanies?

Maybe, because the apostle John tells us that "No one has ever seen God, but the one and only Son, who is himself God and is in closest relationship with the Father, has made him known" (John 1:18, NIV). When God makes an appearance in the Old Testament, then, we can assume that it's Jesus, the Son of God.

How do we know that He did this?

Consider this exchange that Jesus had with the Jewish leaders, who were all for holding on to Abraham but rejecting Jesus. The Lord speaks first here:

"Your father Abraham rejoiced at the thought of seeing my day; he saw it and was glad."

"You are not yet fifty years old," they said to him, "and you have seen Abraham!"

"Very truly I tell you," Jesus answered, "before Abraham was born, I am!"

(John 8:56–58, NIV)

The Lord is indicating that at some point in his life, the patriarch Abraham met Him, in what we call a preincarnate appearance.

For me, the account of the two disciples on the Emmaus road in the gospel of Luke really settles the issue of Jesus' making multiple appearances in the Old Testament. Do you remember that remarkable story?

Now that same day two of them were going to a village called Emmaus, about seven miles from Jerusalem. They were talking with each other about everything that had happened. As they talked and discussed these things with each other, Jesus himself came up and walked along with them; but they were kept from recognizing him.

He asked them, "What are you discussing together as you walk along?"

They stood still, their faces downcast. One of them, named Cleopas, asked him, "Are you the only one visiting Jerusalem who does not know the things that have happened there in these days?"

"What things?" he asked.

"About Jesus of Nazareth," they replied. "He was a prophet, powerful in word and deed before God and all the people. The chief priests and our rulers handed him over to be sentenced to death, and they crucified him; but we had hoped that he was the one who was going to redeem Israel. And what is more, it is the third day since all this took place. In addition, some of our women amazed us. They went to the tomb early this morning but didn't find his body. They came and told us that they had seen a vision of angels, who said he was alive. Then some of our companions went to the tomb and found it just as the women had said, but they did not see Jesus."

He said to them, "How foolish you are, and how slow to believe all that the prophets have spoken! Did not the Messiah have to suffer these things and then enter his glory?" And beginning with Moses and all the Prophets, he explained to them what was said in all the Scriptures concerning himself.

(Luke 24:13–27, NIV)

Wow! Wouldn't you have loved to listen in on *that* conversation? He took them through all of the passages in the Bible that allude to

Messiah: the types, the pictures, and no doubt the Christophanies themselves. I wish someone could have followed about two paces behind that little group, recording them on an iPhone. (And I wish that someone could have been me.) When I get to Heaven, I would definitely love to have a conversation with Jesus just like that one.

Appearing to Abraham

Let's consider some potential Christophanies—appearances of Jesus before Bethlehem. The first I would reference is found in Genesis 22, the story of Abraham and Isaac on Mount Moriah. At the time of this incident, Abraham and Sarah were quite old, yet the Lord revealed to them that they would have a son in their old age.

When the boy was born, they named him Isaac, or "Laughter," because they were filled with joy beyond words. The little boy brought great happiness to their home, and he became the apple of his father's eye.

That is why it almost seemed unimaginable when the Lord came to Abraham in Genesis 22 with a request that must have shaken the old man to his core.

"Abraham!" God called.

"Yes," he replied. "Here I am."

"Take your son, your only son—yes, Isaac, whom you love so much—and go to the land of Moriah. Go and sacrifice him as a burnt offering on one of the mountains, which I will show you." (verses 1–2, NLT)

The Bible says that God was testing Abraham's faith. Had the old patriarch allowed young Isaac to become an idol in his life? Perhaps. It's possible for any of us to allow things or people to become more important to us than God Himself—even a wife or a husband, a son or a daughter.

All of this, of course, was an Old Testament picture of what would happen some two thousand years later at the cross of Calvary, where God would offer His own Son. This passage, then, gives us two views of the same event. It gives us the perspective of Abraham, who was willing to obey God and do what He required. But we can also learn from Isaac's point of view. Isaac was a young man at this point and would have been able to resist his elderly dad, if he chose to. As they were on their journey and nearing the place of sacrifice on the mountain, he might well have realized that they had no animal with them, and that he, Isaac, was going to be the one offered up on that altar.

Realizing that, Isaac could have said, "You know, Dad, I've been thinking about this. I think it makes more sense for *you* to be the sacrifice rather than me. After all, you're old, and I'm young. You've seen your day, but I haven't had much of a chance at life. Why don't we flip this thing around, and I will sacrifice you?"

But Isaac didn't say anything like that. To his credit, he submitted himself to the will of his father, even to the point of being bound and lying on the altar. What trust! And as Abraham raised that knife and was about to bring it down on his own son, the Lord suddenly intervened. In Genesis 22:11–12 we read,

> At that moment the angel of the LORD called to him from heaven, "Abraham! Abraham!"
>
> "Yes," Abraham replied. "Here I am!"
>
> "Don't lay a hand on the boy!" the angel said. "Do not hurt him in any way, for now I know that you truly fear God. You have not withheld from me even your son, your only son." (NLT)

I believe this was a Christophany. The text doesn't refer to just any angel, but to "the angel of the LORD." And notice that He speaks as God, saying, "You have not withheld from *me* even your son, your only son" (emphasis added). I believe this was Jesus Himself intervening at this strategic moment—which was a perfect picture of what He Himself would experience at the cross of Calvary. Abraham was prepared to offer his son, his beloved child of promise. And

Jesus said in John 3:16, "For God so loved the world that He gave His only begotten Son, that whoever believes in Him should not perish but have everlasting life."

A wrestling match with Jacob

Over in Genesis 32, I believe the Bible gives us yet another Christophany, in the account of Jacob wrestling with a visitor from Heaven.

Jacob, the son of Isaac and the grandson of Abraham, found himself alone one momentous night, camping out by the stream called Jabbok. You can read the full story in the Bible, but on this particular night, Jacob was more afraid than he had ever been in his life. He had endured some difficult and bitter years. Now in midlife, he felt like the weight of the world was resting on his shoulders. He feared for his family, he feared the uncertain future that lay ahead of him, and he feared for his very life.

That's where we pick up the story in the Scriptures:

So Jacob was left alone, and a man wrestled with him till daybreak. When the man saw that he could not overpower him, he touched the socket of Jacob's hip so that his hip was wrenched as he wrestled with the man. Then the man said, "Let me go, for it is daybreak."

But Jacob replied, "I will not let you go unless you bless me."

The man asked him, "What is your name?"

"Jacob," he answered.

Then the man said, "Your name will no longer be Jacob, but Israel, because you have struggled with God and with humans and have overcome."

Jacob said, "Please tell me your name."

But he replied, "Why do you ask my name?" Then he blessed him there.

So Jacob called the place Peniel, saying, "It is because I saw God face to face, and yet my life was spared." (verses 24–30, NIV)

I don't think Jacob was wrestling with an angel here; I think Jacob was wrestling with Jesus.

That night began for Jacob in solitude and in an intense prayer time (see verses 9–12). And then Jacob had an up-close-and-personal encounter with Jesus Christ that would change his life.

It's often that way for us, isn't it? Our life circumstances force us into a corner—and perhaps a very frightening, intimidating corner. Do we cry out to God in that moment, or do we try to battle it through on our own, relying on our own strength and wisdom?

That's a very, very important question. In fact, your life may hinge on how you respond in that moment of great fear and pressure.

Jacob turned to the Lord, the God of his father and grandfather. He meant business with God, and God meant business with him.

Obviously, the Lord was never in any danger of being "pinned" in that wrestling match with Jacob. (It would have been like the legendary Hulk Hogan wrestling with a five-year-old.) In the struggle, however, Jacob's hip was wrenched, making him disabled. By the end of the night, he was clinging to the Lord, crying out, "I will not let You go unless You bless me!" Jacob had gone from fighting to submitting, from resisting to resting. And that was what God had been waiting for. He had spent much of his life fighting with God, but in that moment he finally surrendered. As a result, the Lord gave him a new name.

I want you to note what the Lord said to Jacob in verse 28: "You have struggled with God."

Jacob acknowledged that and said, "I have seen God."

I think this is a clear reference to a Christophany, a before-Bethlehem appearance of our Lord Jesus Christ.

Are you wrestling with God? Sometimes in our humanity and in our foolishness, that's what we do. God clearly reveals His will to us, and we say, "But I don't want that. I want my will. I want to do it my way." And we find ourselves wrestling with God through years of our lives. How much better it is when we surrender to His will.

It was Corrie ten Boom who said, "Don't wrestle, just nestle." Don't fight with the One who has your best interests in mind.

A message for Mr. and Mrs. Manoah

Samson's life began with a miracle. The parents of that famous strong man and judge of Israel had been unable to have children, which was a great shame and grief to people in that era.

Then one day, on what was probably a very ordinary day in every other respect, Mrs. Manoah had an amazing visitor:

> The angel of the LORD appeared to Manoah's wife and said, "Even though you have been unable to have children, you will soon become pregnant and give birth to a son. So be careful; you must not drink wine or any other alcoholic drink nor eat any forbidden food. You will become pregnant and give birth to a son, and his hair must never be cut. For he will be dedicated to God as a Nazirite from birth. He will begin to rescue Israel from the Philistines."
>
> The woman ran and told her husband, "A man of God appeared to me! He looked like one of God's angels, terrifying to see. I didn't ask where he was from, and he didn't tell me his name." (Judges 13:3–6, NLT)

Mrs. Manoah wasn't sure of whom she had just seen.

I believe she was seeing Jesus.

Manoah, who hadn't yet seen this mysterious, heavenly visitor, prayed that God would send Him again, and He did. Manoah asked for the visitor's name and received this reply: "Why do you ask My name, seeing it is wonderful?" (verse 18).

After this, Manoah and his wife brought an offering of thanksgiving to the Lord. And as the flame was going up, the Lord ascended into the flame and went up to Heaven. Manoah was immediately seized with panic, crying out, "We shall surely die, because we have seen God!" (verse 22).

Manoah and his wife knew they had seen more than a "man of God" and more than an angel. They knew in their hearts they had seen the living God Himself. And when they asked the visitor His name, He replied that it was "wonderful." Where have we heard that before? In Isaiah 9:6, prophesying the coming of Messiah, we read, "And His name will be called Wonderful, Counselor, Mighty God, Everlasting Father, Prince of Peace."

By the way, the word *wonderful* given to Manoah that day is the same Hebrew word that was used in Isaiah 9:6, and it means "surpassing or beyond human ability to understand."

I find it interesting how the Lord withheld His name from Manoah and did not reveal who He was. That is because in the Old

Testament, Christ is concealed, but in the New Testament, Christ is revealed.

In C. S. Lewis's classic children's novel, *The Voyage of the Dawn Treader*, there is a powerful scene near the end of the book where Aslan the great lion (who symbolizes Christ) tells Lucy and Edmund that they are too old to come back to Narnia and must live out their lives in England.

Through her tears Lucy says, "It isn't Narnia, you know. It's you. We shan't meet you there. And how can we live, never meeting you?"

Aslan replies that they will meet him again and that he is in their world, too.

Then he says, "But there I have another name. . . . This was the very reason why you were brought to Narnia, that by knowing me here for a little, you may know me better there."

In other words, their eyes would be opened, and they would come to know Jesus Himself.

In the story of Manoah, the Lord's identity was concealed. But it has now been revealed in what will become known as the New Covenant.

His presence in the flames

In my opinion, there is another dramatic Christophany in the story of Shadrach, Meshach, and Abed-Nego, three Jewish teenagers who followed the Lord. After the little nation of Judah was conquered by mighty Babylon, many of the Jews were taken into captivity in that enemy city and remained there for seventy years. Nebuchadnezzar, the king of Babylon, singled out the three young men to enter into his service, grooming them to become leaders in the kingdom someday.

He enrolled them in Babylonian university, desiring to school them in all the ways of that twisted, godless culture. One day Nebuchadnezzar had a massive golden image of himself erected, and he commanded everyone in his kingdom to bow down before it and worship—or be put to death. In terror for their lives, all the people obediently fell before this image—except for Shadrach, Meshach, and Abed-Nego.

Refusing to bow, these three young Hebrews stood out like sore thumbs, and their shocking refusal was immediately reported to the king. Outraged, Nebuchadnezzar hauled them into his royal presence and told them they'd better bow down or he would have them thrown into a fiery furnace.

They were polite and respectful, but all three of them made it very clear they would never bow before an image of gold.

Let's pick up the story in the Scriptures:

And these three men, Shadrach, Meshach, and Abed-Nego,

fell down bound into the midst of the burning fiery furnace.

Then King Nebuchadnezzar was astonished; and he rose in haste and spoke, saying to his counselors, "Did we not cast three men bound into the midst of the fire?"

They answered and said to the king, "True, O king."

"Look!" he answered, "I see four men loose, walking in the midst of the fire; and they are not hurt, and the form of the fourth is like the Son of God."

(Daniel 3:23–25)

I believe that was a Christophany—that Jesus Himself was walking with His boys through the fire.

And do you know what? He still does that. Jesus will walk with you through your fire, whatever that fire may be. In Isaiah 43:2–3 we read these words:

When you pass through the waters, I will be with you;
And through the rivers, they shall not overflow you.
When you walk through the fire, you shall not be burned,
Nor shall the flame scorch you.
For I am the LORD your God,
The Holy One of Israel, your Savior.

We are never alone in life.

This is the message we see from Genesis to Revelation. Jesus Christ always has been there. He came to Abraham at the moment of supreme crisis. He came to Jacob when the weight of the world was on that man's shoulders. He came to Samson's parents, who had imagined their situation to be hopeless. He came to the three Hebrew young men in the midst of the flames so they walked through that fire without even getting their robes singed.

Then, in the fullness of time, He came to Earth as a human being—a little baby, placed in a manger of hay. He grew up, clear-eyed and strong, knowing all along there was a cross in His future and that He would lay down His life for your sins and my sins.

Rising from the dead, He is now with us always. In Hebrews 13:5 He says, "I will never leave you nor forsake you." And in Matthew 28:20 He says, "Surely I am with you always, to the very end of the age" (NIV).

2

A TWISTED FAMILY TREE

The song says, "There's no place like home for the holidays."

I agree. I'd rather be home with my little family at Christmas than anywhere else in the world. But "home for Christmas" also can mean getting together with extended family—relatives you don't see (or have to deal with) very often.

And that can be just a little bit stressful.

Let's face it—we all have weird families. We all have that obnoxious uncle, that strange aunt, those twisted cousins. And Grandpa? Well, let's admit it: he's getting just a little bit crazier every year.

Maybe your parents were divorced and so you also have to find yourself contending with half brothers, half sisters, and family members who (if you were honest) really don't seem much like family at all. Maybe you have to go visit your mom and her new boyfriend, or your dad and his new lady, and it's just a little bit awkward.

Or worse yet, they're all coming to your house, and you have to get the place ready, prepare meals, and find spots for everyone to sleep. The following song was written by my friend Dennis Agajanian's father. He called it "Your Relatives Are Coming to Town":

> Well, you'd better give up on Christmas this year
> You haven't a chance with everyone here
> Your relatives are coming to town.
>
> They're bringing their kids to add to your fun
> Staying ten days; you thought it was one
> Your relatives are coming to town.
>
> They will monopolize your bathroom
> And take your solitude
> They will eat you out of house and home
> And complain about your food.
>
> There is only one way to save your Noël—
> Give them your home and rent a motel
> Your relatives are coming to town.

This is the time of year when people can become abnormally stressed out. I remember reading in the newspaper about a guy who had dug out his tree lights and was trying to get things sorted out so his family could decorate. The problem was that his wife had left the lights in a great big tangled ball the year before, and that made him angry. He had to set the mess down on the driveway to go into the house for something, and while his back was turned, his teenage daughter pulled in and drove over the lights.

He freaked out and started screaming, "Can't you see? I am trying to put up the Christmas lights!"

And then he told his wife he was going to go let off a little bit of steam. So he went into the backyard and started firing off rounds from his .45 caliber pistol. He was arrested for reckless endangerment and ended up in jail (which didn't improve his mood at all).

Just a couple of days ago, I read about a man in Rock Springs, Wyoming, who made the mistake of opening his Christmas present too early. Infuriated that he couldn't wait, his wife stabbed him with a kitchen knife.

Ah . . . those family troubles!

Frankly, we all have them. And the person who says they don't is either delusional or outright lying. No one comes from a perfect family, because families are made up of flawed, fallible human beings.

Every now and then I hear people say, "Oh, I came from a dysfunctional home."

I have to bite my tongue to keep from saying, "Will you get over that, already?" We *all* came from dysfunctional homes. Every one of us. I came from a dysfunctional home. Now I am the head of a dysfunctional home. What did you expect—that you would have parents like the Cleavers? More likely they resemble the Simpsons.

Dr. Ian Cook, director of the UCLA depression research program, said this about the Christmas season: "Some people have unreasonable expectations—the holidays have to be happy."[1]

Sometimes at Christmas we're presented with ideal pictures of ideal families sitting together in ideal living rooms as they watch the snow fall outside and sing carols together. And then we feel as though we've fallen short because our families just don't look like that. Well, guess what? No family does! Very few families today even slightly resemble those in the old movies. But that doesn't mean we can't build some good memories.

The fact is that none of us has the perfect family. Every family has its share of problems, skeletons, dysfunctions, weird dynamics, and eccentric relatives.

It's popular these days to go digging into your family tree, maybe using one of those handy computer programs that assists you in chasing down all the roots, branches, and twigs. I have a friend who's really into this, and every time I see him, he's made some new discovery about his heritage that he wants to tell me about.

There's nothing wrong with pursuing this as a hobby, as long as you remember that it works both ways. You might discover that you're related to some famous general or president or famous person. And you also might find out that your great-grandma was a madam or that your grandfather's uncle was hung for being a horse thief.

The human family has as many bad apples as good ones—probably more! So what if you were researching your ancestors online and discovered that you had a number of prostitutes populating your family tree? Is that something you'd want to tell people about?

Your friend might say, "Hey, I found out that I'm a direct descendent of George Washington."

Another friend might counter, "Well, I found out that I have royal blood flowing in my family."

And you would say, "I discovered that we have three prostitutes in our family tree."

Is that something you would be proud of?

Why do I bring that up? Because as we begin to delve into the most famous family tree in human history—the family tree of Jesus Christ Himself—we find liars, cheats, adulterers, and prostitutes. The Lord's family tree had some of the most notable sinners ever, so He knows all about having some relatives that might embarrass you. Jesus knows all about dysfunctional family situations. So if you think you are alone in having problems this Christmas, you can know for sure that it's simply not the case.

But we will also see something else at work in the family tree of our Lord: grace—incredible, restoring, wonderful grace, the unmerited favor of God.

Sometimes you and I might look at our lives, sigh deeply, shake our heads, and say, "I don't think God could ever use me. I've made too many mistakes, and I don't see how anything good could come out of the mess I've made of my life."

This story, among other things, shows that is simply not the case. The grace of God is clearly on display here.

THE STORY BEFORE THE STORY

When we tell the Christmas story, we usually cut to the chase. By that I mean we go to the beautiful narratives found in Matthew, and especially in the gospel of Luke, and revel at the story of the birth of Jesus. When we do that, we often skip over the information that immediately precedes the story. And what precedes the story in the gospel of Matthew is a lengthy list of names—a genealogy.

Why do we skip it? For one thing, the Jewish names sound strange to our ears and are difficult to pronounce. For another thing, it simply doesn't mean that much to us; it doesn't seem to relate to our lives.

Genealogies were a big deal to the Jewish people for a number of reasons. Through these long lists of ancestral names, a family could determine whether they were related to anyone in the priesthood or to someone who happened to be in the royal line. The genealogy might also figure into family inheritance issues. So the Jews loved those long lists of names, dating them back as far as they could go.

The genealogy in Matthew 1, however, affects every one of us. What's more, it's as inspired by God as any other passage in the entire Bible. Let's dip into it together:

> The book of the genealogy of Jesus Christ, the Son of David, the Son of Abraham:
>
> Abraham begot Isaac, Isaac begot Jacob, and Jacob begot Judah and his brothers. Judah begot Perez and Zerah by Tamar, Perez begot Hezron, and Hezron begot Ram. Ram begot Amminadab, Amminadab begot Nahshon, and Nahshon begot Salmon. Salmon begot Boaz by Rahab, Boaz begot Obed by Ruth, Obed begot Jesse, and Jesse begot David the king.
>
> David the king begot Solomon by her who had been the wife of Uriah. (verses 1–6)

The mother referred to in that last verse was Bathsheba. Now drop down to verse 13:

> Zerubbabel begot Abiud, Abiud begot Eliakim, and Eliakim begot Azor. Azor begot Zadok, Zadok begot Achim, and

Achim begot Eliud. Eliud begot Eleazar, Eleazar begot Matthan, and Matthan begot Jacob. And Jacob begot Joseph the husband of Mary, of whom was born Jesus who is called Christ. (verses 13–16)

When you take the time to look into it, you discover there are some pretty amazing names in this lineup. Normally Jewish genealogies didn't include women; in this genealogy, there are five. When you really find out who some of these people are and what they did, it begins to read like a biblical soap opera. As I said, it certainly gives hope to those of us who have experienced disappointing failures in our lives. In this genealogy, the prelude to the Christmas story, we see God, in His mercy, doing for sinners what they could never do for themselves. We see the love and grace of God mending broken lives and gently piecing together shattered hopes.

This is why Jesus came.

Some people think Jesus came to Earth to make good people just a little bit better or to give us a cause to celebrate and experience deeper happiness and peace. Those are fine things, and the Lord certainly can accomplish such outcomes in our lives.

But that is not why He came.

The reason He came was that we were irreparably separated from God by our sin. As the apostle Paul wrote, we were "without hope and without God in the world" (Ephesians 2:12, NIV). The message of the coming Savior was, "You shall call His name JESUS, for He will save His people from their sins" (Matthew 1:21). Christmas is about God's solution for sin. Jesus didn't come to Earth to make good people better; Jesus came to reach out to people who have made a mess of their lives. Jesus came to heal broken lives and to restore shattered hopes.

The book of Galatians tells us,

> But when the right time came, God sent his Son, born of a woman, subject to the law. God sent him to buy freedom for us who were slaves to the law, so that he could adopt us as his very own children. And because we are his children, God has sent the Spirit of his Son into our hearts, prompting us to call out, "Abba, Father." (4:4–6, NLT)

Jesus came to redeem us.

Don't let that word *redeem* throw you. It simply means "to buy back" and was used of an individual who would buy back a slave who was up for auction in the slave market. That is what Jesus did. He saw us in the slave market of sin, paid the price for our freedom, and set us free from the power of sin and the ultimate penalty of sin. That is the *real* message of Christmas.

Jesus came to put broken lives back together. As He began His ministry, He stood in the synagogue of His hometown, Nazareth, and read these words from the Scriptures, pertaining to Himself: "The Spirit of the LORD is upon Me, because He has anointed Me to preach the gospel to the poor; He has sent Me to heal the broken-hearted, to proclaim liberty to the captives and recovery of sight to the blind, to set at liberty those who are oppressed" (Luke 4:18).

Jesus has come to heal your broken heart. Do you have a broken heart? Do you have a shattered life? Do you have a mess on your hands, and you can't blame anyone but yourself? Or could it be that you are living in a mess created by someone else, and it seems so unfair? Jesus has come to put these things back together again.

The gospel of Matthew emphasizes the fact that Jesus fulfilled the prophecies of the Old Testament concerning the coming Messiah. Part of the evidence Matthew used to demonstrate that fact is the genealogy in the first chapter that traces Jesus' lineage to the royal line of David. Why is that important? Because the Bible said that the Messiah would come from the root and the offspring of David. Any claimant to the throne of Israel had to demonstrate, through his genealogy, that he descended from David and was in the line of royalty.

We have two genealogies given to us in the Gospels: one in Matthew and the other in Luke. These represent Jesus' paternal genealogy (Matthew) and His maternal genealogy (Luke). In other words, Matthew's genealogy traces Jesus through Joseph's line, while Luke traces Him through Mary's. And both trace Him back to David.

That is why Mary and Joseph had to go to Bethlehem to pay the tax demanded by Caesar. Bethlehem was the boyhood home of David before he ascended the throne. It was a legal necessity for them to return to David's ancestral home to pay their tax, but it also was a direct fulfillment of Micah 5:2:

But you, Bethlehem Ephrathah,

Though you are little among the thousands of Judah,

Yet out of you shall come forth to Me

The One to be Ruler in Israel,

Whose goings forth are from of old,

From everlasting.

It's important to notice that Matthew doesn't refer to Joseph as the father of Jesus. The text refers to him as "the husband of Mary, of whom was born Jesus who is called Christ" (Matthew 1:16). The Scriptures are abundantly clear in pointing out that Jesus was not the son of Joseph. Joseph was the husband of Mary and became a father figure and a guardian to Jesus. Jesus' Father was and literally is God, who caused the birth of our Lord to take place supernaturally from the womb of the virgin by the power of the Holy Spirit. Because

Jesus had no human father, He couldn't be a descendent of David's, except through His mother. Be that as it may, the legal right to rule always came through the father's side. In Jesus' case, He legally was Joseph's oldest son.

INTERESTING CHARACTERS ON THE FAMILY TREE

David

Plucked from obscurity, David became the greatest king in the history of the nation of Israel. The Bible calls David "a man after [God's] own heart" (1 Samuel 13:14). His name is usually associated with two other names that describe both his greatest victory and his greatest, most tragic defeat.

On the victory side, who could forget Goliath, the nine-foot-six-inch Philistine warrior whom David killed in the Valley of Elah with only a sling and a stone? I was telling this story to my granddaughter a number of years ago and showing her how Goliath fell. So I said, "You be David," which of course meant that she got to throw the stone—only we didn't use stones; we used pillows. So I fell forward, just like Goliath, and crashed on the bed. Then she was the giant, and I got to be David and smack her with the pillow. (I'm sure it was all very instructive for her.)

Goliath was David's greatest victory.

On the defeat side, we remember the sorrow and anguish caused by David's adultery with Bathsheba, the wife of his loyal warrior and friend, Uriah the Hittite. David not only stole a man's wife, but he also stole a man's life. He deliberately had Uriah killed in battle in an attempt to cover up his sin with Bathsheba and the resulting pregnancy.

And yet the royal line originates with David, and Jesus Himself would be called "the son of David." Despite his sin, David made it into the most exclusive family tree in human history.

Abraham

In Matthew 1:2 we read about Abraham, a very great man in Jewish history who is considered the father of the Jews and the father of the faith. But he also had flaws and shortcomings. We know that he lied (twice) about the identity of his wife, Sarah, trying to pass her off as his sister. He did it because she was a beautiful woman, and Abraham wanted to protect his own skin in case a powerful ruler went after her. This demonstrated not only deception and cowardice, but a lack of faith in the God who had called him and led him through the land of Canaan.

In spite of these things, however, God established Abraham as the father of the Jewish people and put him clearly in the messianic line.

Tamar

How in the world did this woman end up in the Lord's family tree? Quite honestly, I'm surprised by that. Her sordid story is told in Genesis 38. As you read her story of prostitution and deception, you will be hard-pressed to find anything of redeeming value. She is pretty much a corrupt character, with not much of a silver lining. Yet amazingly, by the grace of God, she ends up being an ancestress of the Messiah Himself.

Rahab

Speaking of prostitutes, Tamar had to play the part of a prostitute once, to obtain her goal. But Rahab was a regular professional. Her house of ill repute was known by everyone in the city of Jericho. Tamar resorted to prostitution to obtain a certain end, but Rahab did it for money. What's more, she also was a Gentile, a Canaanite. When the Israelite army sent spies into Jericho to scope out the city before an impending attack, Rahab hid them in her home and was subsequently blessed as a result.

We speak of "Rahab the harlot," and somehow that doesn't sound so bad. But we could also say, "Rahab the prostitute" or "Rahab the hooker." That is what she was. And yet because she did this act of kindness toward the people of God, she and her family were spared when Jericho was conquered. Even more surprising, she was brought into the messianic line as the wife of Salmon and the mother of the godly Boaz, David's great-grandfather.

Ruth

Like Tamar and Rahab, Ruth was a Gentile. She married one of two sons born to a woman named Naomi. They were both Jewish boys, Mahlon and Chilion, whose names meant "sickly" and "pining."

True to their names, both of these brothers died, leaving two young Moabite widows. Naomi's husband also died.

When brokenhearted Naomi decided to return to Judah from the land of Moab, she told her two widowed daughters-in-law that they would do better if they stayed in Moab. One of the women took her advice and turned back, but the other, Ruth, refused to leave Naomi's side. When the older woman tried to send her away, Ruth spoke words that would go down in history to this day, saying,

> Entreat me not to leave you,
> Or to turn back from following after you;
> For wherever you go, I will go;
> And wherever you lodge, I will lodge;
> Your people shall be my people,
> And your God, my God. (Ruth 1:16)

It was a wonderful affirmation of Ruth's loyal heart. But what makes it all so remarkable is that Ruth was a Moabite, a woman of Moab, one of Israel's worst enemies. Where did the Moabites come from? They were the result of the incestuous relations between Lot and his two unmarried daughters. The son produced by Lot's union with his older daughter was Moab—the father of the Moabites.

It starts to sound like some tacky reality show on TV. And yet here is this pagan woman from Moab, Israel's ancestral enemy, who came to faith in God and married Boaz. In so doing, she became the grandmother of David, Israel's greatest king.

Bathsheba

It's interesting to note that in Matthew's genealogy, she is identified only as "the wife of Uriah." Even in the messianic line, though she is included, we are reminded that she was the wife of another. David the king begot Solomon by "her who had been the wife of Uriah" (1:6).

Some commentators place all the blame on David for that affair with Bathsheba, but I think she comes in for a share of blame as well. As they say, "It takes two to tango," and maybe she shouldn't have been bathing where David could see her, in plain sight of the palace. After the sin took place, she also cooperated in the cover-up that went on for a long time.

Even so, God extended His grace to her and included her as well in the messianic line.

To me, that is one of the great values of Matthew, chapter 1. We can look at the names of the people listed in the messianic line and just let ourselves be blown away by the grace of God. This is a God who can take the darkest, most twisted, and unhappiest of life stories and bring something good out of it, for His glory. No matter what your family background is or how you came into being, God has a plan and a purpose for your life.

Let me illustrate. The McDaniel clan, my family on my mother's side, originally came from Scotland, settling mostly in Arkansas. And then some of them, including my mother, came out to California. As you might know, if you've read my story, I was born out of wedlock. I was the result of a one-night stand that my mom had with some sailor she met in Long Beach.

I don't have a beautiful family tree that I can point to. Looking back on my McDaniel ancestors, it seems like they were either notorious sinners or notorious Christians. We had a lot of alcoholics and more than our share of tragedy in our family background. And my father's background? I don't even know what it was because I don't know my father.

So here I am, not planned, and conceived out of wedlock. Yet *God* had a plan for my life, and He chose me to be His child. And He has a plan for your life as well.

I am a child of God today because of God's grace. Period. The

Bible says, "For by grace you have been saved through faith, and that not of yourselves; it is the gift of God, not of works, lest anyone should boast. For we are His workmanship, created in Christ Jesus for good works, which God prepared beforehand that we should walk in them" (Ephesians 2:8–10).

We are reminded that even if we fail like Abraham or David, like Rahab or Tamar or Bathsheba, there is still hope. God can take the broken pieces of our lives and put them back together.

Maybe your life is in something of a mess right now. Your family might be falling apart, or perhaps you have sinned in some area of your life. Know this: God can take this mess and bring about transformation. He can turn the broken pieces into something beautiful . . . a masterpiece.

WHAT WE LEARN FROM THE GENEALOGY OF JESUS

1. We see the grace of God richly displayed.

The stories of the four women in the list in Matthew 1 aren't included so that you can focus on their sin; they are included so that you can marvel over the incomparable grace of God. Yes, other Scripture passages describe their shortcomings in detail. But they are included in *this* list to show God's kindness and grace being extended.

That doesn't mean we should minimize or celebrate sin or imagine that we can disobey God without facing consequences. As the apostle Paul said in Romans 6, "What shall we say, then? Shall we go on sinning so that grace may increase? [Or overflow or, literally, go down the drain.] By no means! We are those who have died to sin; how can we live in it any longer?" (verses 1–2, NIV).

Everyone faces repercussions for their sin. David faced repercussions. So did Tamar. Nevertheless, we are reminded that God is truly a forgiving God and will give us second chances to obey Him and serve Him. That is the grace of God on display.

Maybe you have made some wrong choices too. You need to come to the Lord and say, "Father, I have failed. Would You redeem those failures? Will You redeem my life and bring something good, something of value, in spite of the wrong I have done?"

He has done that over and over again for millions of people, and He will do it for you.

2. The focus of this family tree in the Scriptures is on Jesus, not on His family.

As I look at the Lord's family and His ancestors, I say to myself, "Wow. His family was messed up like mine is." But the effect of looking at these failing, fallible people in the Lord's family tree also causes me to say, "This is a God who is approachable. This is a God who can understand where I come from and what I struggle with. This is a God whom I can *know*."

For many people today, the God of the Bible seems too good to be true. Jesus seems like a one-dimensional figure in stained glass—and a million miles from real life with all its pains and troubles and complications.

When I was a little boy, I went to live with my grandparents for a time, and I accompanied my grandmother to church on Sunday. I didn't understand most of what I heard and saw. But I remember that in my grandmother's home, she had a painting of Jesus—a familiar depiction of Him that was very popular in the 1950s. I'm sure you've seen it and may even have it in your home. In this particular depiction of Christ, He is turned away, looking somewhere off into the distance. He isn't looking at you; His attention is elsewhere.

I remember looking at that picture of Jesus and thinking to myself, *I would like to know that Jesus—but I don't think I can know Him. Besides, He isn't interested in me. He isn't even looking at me in the picture.*

That is how I felt about God—that He was busy, preoccupied, and didn't really care about someone like Greg Laurie. Maybe you have thought of God as angry or disappointed in you, as someone who is always ready to come down on you because you don't measure up. Both of those impressions are false.

The authentic flesh-and-blood Jesus of the Bible was in touch with the real world. He came from a real family with lots of problems, yet He Himself was without sin. Jesus became a part of the human family so that we might become a part of the heavenly family. He has walked in your shoes and understands your life situation, no matter how twisted up and complicated it may seem to you, better than you know it yourself.

Though Jesus was without sin Himself, He loved sinners. In fact, His enemies called Him a friend of sinners (see Matthew 11:19; Luke 7:34), and I don't think He minded that at all. He was tested in all points as we are and yet was without sin (see Hebrews 4:15). And Hebrews 7:25 tells us that "he is able, once and forever, to save those who come to God through him. He lives forever to intercede with God on their behalf" (NLT).

3. We have this family tree in the Scriptures so that we might have hope for our future and the future of our families.

While you may not have murderers or prostitutes in your family tree, you surely have some adulterers, liars, and cheats. No family would be complete without them. But Jesus can intervene in your life, just as it is.

Allow me to offer this word of caution. It has been said that an ounce of prevention is better than a pound of cure. What state is your family in right now? If you are the man of the family, are you a good spiritual leader? I have found that in far too many Christian homes, the woman—the wife and mother—is the spiritual leader, the initiator of all things spiritual.

She is the one who says, "Come on, let's get up and go to church. Let's get going." Or she will be the one to say, "Let's read a little bit of the Bible together." Or perhaps, "Let's pray about this. Let's take it to the Lord."

All too often, it is the man—the husband and father—who drags his feet or finds an excuse not to do those things. In many cases, then, the man is passive at best about spiritual things. In some situations, he actually drags his family down, saying things like, "I don't want to go to church. Why don't you stay home with me?"

That's what this family tree in the Scriptures reminds me of. Someday someone will be looking at your place in the family. Will they say, "Just skip over that name," as if you weren't even there or had no influence at all? Or will they pause by your name and say, "This was a godly man. This man loved the Lord and encouraged his family in the Lord."

So if you are the man of the house, what I'm saying right now is that you need to step up and take some spiritual initiative and leadership.

"Well, Greg," you say, "it's too late for that. I've made a lot of mistakes and missed a lot of opportunities."

Welcome to the club! So have all of us. As long as you are drawing breath, however, it is not too late to have an influence on your loved ones by the example you set. God bless your wife, and thank the Lord for her interest in spiritual things. But it's time for you to be a man and take some spiritual leadership. It's time for you to be loving your wife as Christ loves His church (see Ephesians 5:25–33).

If you are a woman and a wife reading these words, you're not off the hook! You are to love your husband. When was the last time you told him how much you appreciate everything he does for you and the family? He knows all about the things you don't like about him and where you think he's falling short. Maybe it's time that you affirmed him as the spiritual leader in your home. When he takes even a baby step in that direction, respond with encouragement.

What kind of parent are you right now? Are you raising your children in the "training and instruction of the Lord" (Ephesians 6:4, NIV)? You should be able to say to your sons and daughters, "Not only live by what I teach you, *but live the way that I live. Do what I do.*"

Newsflash: You will fall short and make mistakes. When you do, it's a good thing to go to your kids and say, "Guess what? Dad blew it." "Mom fell short." "I made a mistake. I was out of bounds just now, and I want to ask for your forgiveness."

Does that mean you will lose some authority and respect by humbling yourself like that? No, you will gain their respect as you show them how a man of God or a woman of God owns up to mistakes and relies on the Lord for help. In fact, your children will model your behavior and will be more willing to admit their faults and ask for forgiveness as well.

It is so tragic when we see the sins of the parents visited on their children and the bad behavior of one generation being picked up by the next one—and the next one and the next. That certainly happens, and we all can point to examples in our own experience. Nevertheless, the Lord can step in, intervene, and change things, if we give Him that opportunity.

Maybe you have a prodigal son or daughter. My own son Christopher, now with the Lord, didn't always walk with Christ, though he was raised in a Christian home by parents who loved him with all their hearts. There was a time for a number of years when Christopher went astray. He never stopped believing in God, and he was never disrespectful to his mother or me, but he just went his own way. At one point, after he came back to the Lord, he said to a friend of mine, "One of the reasons I came back again was because I knew that my parents loved me unconditionally." Later, he recommitted his life to Christ and became a Christian husband and father.

If you have a child who has gone astray, just let that child know you love him or her—and keep the porch light on and the door open. Perhaps God, in His mercy, would even use this Christmas season to bring about some reconciliation in your home. If not this year, then perhaps next. Keep praying, and keep holding on to hope.

Sons and daughters are part of that family tree and have responsibilities as well. Ephesians 6:1-3 says, "Children, obey your parents in the Lord, for this is right. 'Honor your father and mother . . . that it may go well with you'" (NIV). If you are a son—even an adult son—*when did you last call your mother?* If you are a daughter, when is the last time you let your dad know how much you appreciate him?

We all have our part to play in the family tree!

Sometimes Christmas, with all its family pressure, is the time when some of our relationship problems come to the surface. So be it! Instead of running from those difficulties or trying to sweep them under the rug, you need to bring the matters before the Lord and then (with His help) deal with them. Why not let Christmas be a time of healing and new closeness rather than tension and unhappiness?

Your marriage, of course, is your most important relationship besides your relationship with God. Is it holding strong? Fraying around the edges? Even beginning to unravel? If you have even contemplated divorce, let me plead with you: Don't get a divorce. Reconcile. Give it another chance. Remember that your decision won't affect your lives only but also the lives of the generations that follow you.

Are you a single person? Remain pure. Don't start a family unintentionally. Wait for that right man or right woman whom God has prepared for you. And if you have messed up, come to the Lord and say, "Lord, here it is. Here is my mistake. Here is my sin. Here is my shortcoming. I am asking You to redeem these things, Lord. I am asking You to intervene. I am asking You to bring beauty out of ashes, as only You can."

Then watch what the Lord can do.

If you struggle with doubts about how He can work, look again at His own family tree. Remember Rahab the prostitute, Tamar, who seduced her own father-in-law, and David, who committed adultery and took the life of a loyal friend. If the Lord could redeem these situations, bringing back all of those names to a position of honor and blessing, then He can do the same thing in your family tree.

3

CHRISMAS, THE PREQUEL

I remember waiting in line at the theater back in 1980 to see *The Empire Strikes Back*, the second movie in the original Star Wars trilogy.

At that point, I didn't have a clue about the plot line. And then some joker who had been in the previous showing walked by with a smirk and said in a loud voice, "Oh, by the way, Darth Vader is Luke's father!"

Every head in the line jerked around, and we all said, "Noooo!"

Those first three Star Wars movies were really good. But then the creator, George Lucas, came up with the idea of doing a series of three prequels. Instead of advancing the story, he moved the story back in time, revealing where Luke Skywalker and Obi-Wan Kenobi came from—and how Darth Vader ended up on the dark side.

Lucas lost me with those movies. I couldn't get into the lizard-faced character of Jar Jar Binks, and I didn't like the prequels at all. Now that Disney has picked up the franchise, I'm hoping we can get on with the original story line and find out what happened to Han Solo, Luke Skywalker, and Princess Leia.

Some prequels—the stories behind the stories—aren't as interesting as the original accounts. But that isn't true of the story of Christmas. Not at all! The main story, of course, begins with the angel coming to Mary, a virgin, and announcing that she would bear a child who would be called "the Son of God." Then there was the birth in Bethlehem, the shepherds, the angelic choir, and later, the wise men following a star.

We love that true story of our Lord's birth, and I, for one, never weary of reading it, hearing about it, singing about it, or just thinking about it.

But in the gospel of Luke there is a prequel to the main story—and it's every bit as good.

THE DOCTOR'S JOURNAL

Luke wasn't one of our Lord's disciples. Because of that, he wasn't an eyewitness to the events he recorded in his gospel, as Matthew and John were. It was Luke's desire to capture an overview of the life of Jesus that would be understandable to those outside the Jewish faith and culture. So with educated skill and a physician's attention to detail—not to mention the heart and artistry of a poet—Dr. Luke gave us highlights from the life of Jesus.

Luke's account is addressed to a man named Theophilus. The only thing we really know about this individual is that his name means "lover of God." Presumably, then, he was a believer. It's just speculation, but he might have been the one who underwrote the project, funding Luke's research as the doctor traveled here and there doing interviews, engaging in conversations, and seeking pertinent details.

In his prologue Luke wrote,

> Many have undertaken to draw up an account of the things that have been fulfilled among us, just as they were handed down to us by those who from the first were eyewitnesses and servants of the word. With this in mind, since I myself have carefully investigated everything from the beginning, I too decided to write an orderly account for you, most excellent Theophilus, so that you may know the certainty of the things you have been taught. (Luke 1:1–4, NIV)

I really like that word *certainty*. Luke believed that if the essence of this true story was set down in an accurate and orderly way, the result would create new believers in Jesus. And he has been so right, as the last two-thousand-plus years have revealed.

In my experience, I've seen many people reject the message

of Christ without even looking into it to see if it might be true.

"Are you a Christian?" you may ask someone.

"No," they reply.

"Have you ever read the Bible?"

"No."

"Have you ever read the New Testament—or even one of the Gospels?"

"No."

"Would you be interested in hearing about Jesus?"

"No."

The fact is they have decided to reject something they know nothing about.

Luke was saying, "I want to put together this orderly account of the Lord's life so that you can know your faith is built on a sure foundation. I want you to know with certainty that these things are true."

Already at this time, there were false stories going around about the birth of Jesus and His life and ministry. I don't know if they had tabloids in their markets in those days (the *Jerusalem Enquirer*?), but there certainly were myths and legends floating around. Dr. Luke wanted to set the record straight, giving an accurate presentation of who Jesus was, what He did, and what He said.

And here is how Luke began his account.

"IN THE DAYS OF HEROD"

There was in the days of Herod, the king of Judea, a certain priest named Zacharias, of the division of Abijah. His wife was of the daughters of Aaron, and her name was Elizabeth. And they were both righteous before God, walking in all the commandments and ordinances of the Lord blameless. But they had no child, because Elizabeth was barren, and they were both well advanced in years.

So it was, that while he was serving as priest before God in the order of his division, according to the custom of the priesthood, his lot fell to burn incense when he went into the temple of the Lord. And the whole multitude of the people was praying outside at the hour of incense. Then an angel of the Lord appeared to him, standing on the right side of the altar of incense. And when Zacharias saw him, he was troubled, and fear fell upon him.

But the angel said to him, "Do not be afraid, Zacharias, for your prayer is heard; and your wife Elizabeth will bear you a son, and you shall call his name John. And you will have joy and gladness, and many will rejoice at his birth. For he will be great in the sight of the Lord, and shall drink neither wine nor strong drink. He will also be filled with the

Holy Spirit, even from his mother's womb. And he will turn many of the children of Israel to the Lord their God. He will also go before Him in the spirit and power of Elijah, 'to turn the hearts of the fathers to the children,' and the disobedient to the wisdom of the just, to make ready a people prepared for the Lord." (Luke 1:5-17)

When Luke wrote, "In the days of Herod," it would be like saying in Germany, "In the days of Adolf Hitler" or in China, "In the days of Mao Tse-tung" or in Iraq, "In the days of Saddam Hussein." Those words would give immediate context to the people who actually lived in those places and times. In each case, those were dark and wicked days. For Israel, also suffering under the brutal heel of Roman rule, it was almost as difficult as their days of bondage in Egypt under Pharaoh.

King Herod was in charge, a puppet king under Roman rule, to whom Caesar had given the title "king of the Jews." Herod was known for his sadistic cruelty, fueled as it was by over-the-top paranoia and jealousy. According to historical accounts, this king in name only murdered his wife, her brother, her mother, and several of his own sons, fearing they would present some threat to his rule. It was this Herod who gave the decree to kill all the baby boys, two years old and under, in the vicinity of Bethlehem. One of the popular expressions of the day was, "Better to be one of Herod's pigs than a member of his family."

This was the depressing backdrop of Luke's story. To make matters much worse, the people of Israel had not heard from God for four hundred years. In four centuries, there had not been a single prophet, a single miracle, or a single angelic appearance. Heaven had gone silent, and the prophetic gift had seemingly dried up. Luke's narrative, then, found Israel in the midst of a long night of spiritual darkness.

Even so, God had ended the Old Testament with a promise. In the book of Malachi, the closing book of the Old Testament, God had said,

> But to you who fear My name
> The Sun of Righteousness shall arise
> With healing in His wings;
> And you shall go out
> And grow fat like stall-fed calves. (4:2)

God was saying to the faithful in Israel, "A better day is coming. Though it's dark now, the sun will rise again and bring healing." Bible commentator R. Kent Hughes put it this way: "The great plans of God Almighty, laid in eternal ages past, would begin to unfold as angels rushed to set the stage for the coming dawn."[1]

Not only had God promised that a better day was coming, not only had God promised that a Messiah was coming, but He also had told them they could watch for a forerunner who would announce the arrival of the Messiah and prepare the way for Him. In Malachi 3:1 the Lord said, " 'I will send my messenger, who will prepare the way before me. Then suddenly the Lord you are seeking will come to his temple; the messenger of the covenant, whom you desire, will come,' says the LORD Almighty" (NIV).

When John the Baptist, the "messenger" of this passage, arrived on the scene, he effectively was the bridge between the Old and New Testaments. In a sense, he was the last of the Old Testament prophets heralding the arrival of Israel's long-awaited Messiah.

Sometimes people will talk about "the God of the Old Testament" and "the God of the New Testament," as though He were separate beings. We're told that the God of the Old Testament is harsh, judgmental, and intolerant. The God of the New Testament, however, is compassionate, loving, and accepting. But this whole comparison isn't true at all. The God of the Old Testament and the God of the New Testament is the same God. The Scriptures give us one continuous revelation of God from Genesis through all sixty-six books of the Bible, culminating in the book of Revelation.

John the Baptist bridges the gap between the Old and New Testaments.

Israel longed for the Messiah. Israel longed for someone to deliver them.

A CRITICAL ENCOUNTER

That's the background Dr. Luke gives for the moment when the godly old priest Zacharias went into the temple of the Lord to burn incense. Here is a description of that critical moment in Israel's history from a different Bible translation:

> The crowded congregation outside was praying at the actual time of the incense-burning, when an angel of the Lord appeared on the right side of the incense-altar. When Zacharias saw him, he was terribly agitated and a sense of awe swept over him. But the angel spoke to him, "Do not be afraid, Zacharias; your prayers have been heard. Elisabeth your wife will bear you a son, and you are to call him John." (Luke 1:10–13, PH)

Was this a big deal?

Yes, it was a very big deal. Because the angel who showed up in that moment was none other than Gabriel.

Remember, it had been four hundred years since any angel had made an appearance in Israel. When God finally sent a heavenly messenger, He didn't send just any angel who happened to be on call at the moment. He sent a mega-angel. This is the same Gabriel, one of only two named holy angels in the Scriptures, who had appeared to the prophet Daniel to give him a message about the future Messiah. There is no question that this mighty servant of God is uniquely connected to the life and ministry of Jesus. It was Gabriel who would later appear to Mary, telling her that she is to bear a Son and call His name Jesus.

It is interesting that the last appearance of an angel in the Old Testament came to Zechariah the prophet, and the first angelic appearance of the New Testament also comes to someone named Zechariah, or Zacharias. The name means "God remembers."

Zacharias and his wife, Elizabeth, were an elderly couple who had been, up to that point, childless. Elizabeth's name means "God is an oath" or "my God is an oath." In effect, God would confirm both of their names, fulfilling the very meanings of what their names spoke of.

He was going to keep His oath.

He was going to remember His promise.

WHAT WE CAN LEARN FROM ZACHARIAS AND ELIZABETH

What truths can we take away from this godly couple through whom God worked in that amazing moment of transition in Israel? Here are a few principles we might consider.

1. Zacharias was a humble man.

Contrast him with the wicked and powerful Herod, who would in time be cut down. Zacharias was a humble servant of the Lord. What does it mean to be humble? It *doesn't* mean that you walk around with your hands folded and your eyes cast down, saying, "I'm just a humble man" or "I'm just a humble woman."

That isn't humility—that just means you're being a wimp! A humble person is a strong individual who keeps that strength under control. We see the same idea communicated in the word *meekness*, which means "great power under constraint." (Think of a mighty war horse being controlled by a bit and bridle.)

Zacharias was humble before God, and God favored him, just as we read in James 4:6, where the apostle says, "God resists the proud, but gives grace to the humble." A humble person is simply someone who sees himself as he really is—a sinner in need of a Savior.

Zacharias was a country priest. It was almost like being a

country pastor of a little congregation in some tiny community. To be a country priest meant that he had a modest-sized flock that he would watch over. The priest would represent God to the people, interpret the Scriptures for them, pray for them, counsel them, and render judgment when necessary.

In a real way, each one of us are priests today.

You say, "What do you mean, Greg? I don't keep any clerical collars in my bedroom closet."

Perhaps not, but the Bible tells us in 1 Peter 2: 9 that we are "a chosen generation, a royal priesthood, a holy nation, His own special people, that you may proclaim the praises of Him who called you out of darkness into His marvelous light." Now Jesus is our High Priest, and we are all in the priesthood. It means that we, in essence, *represent God to people*.

Have you thought about it?

God has chosen you as His personal representative. You represent God to the world. You represent God to your city, school, work site, sports team, or neighborhood. You represent God to your family. If you are married, you represent God to your spouse.

I can hear someone say, "That's a lot of pressure, Greg."

Yes, it is.

But that's what being a Christian is all about. The fact is that you are the only Bible some people will ever read. A Christian is a walking epistle, written by God and read by people. The New Testament expresses it like this: "You yourselves are our letter . . . known and read by everyone. You show that you are a letter from Christ, the result of our ministry, written not with ink but with the Spirit of the living God, not on tablets of stone but on tablets of human hearts" (2 Corinthians 3:2–3, NIV). Some of the people you rub shoulders with may never have looked up John 3:16 in a New Testament, but they will read your life. Count on it!

They will watch the way you treat your husband or wife.

They will watch the way you live as a single person.

They will watch the way you transact your business.

They will watch the way you respond to trials and crises in your life.

And they will make evaluations about God according to your lifestyle.

"But that isn't right!" you say. "I don't want that responsibility. I don't want people to do that."

Nevertheless, they will.

2. Zacharias was a faithful man.

As the story begins, we see this humble country priest just going about his duty. Back in those days, each priest would leave his local area and go to Jerusalem to serve in the temple twice a year for one week. I can imagine that this would be something they would really look forward to. You have your little rural parish, but twice a year, you get to serve in the big city of Jerusalem and offer prayers for the nation and its people. And talk about a privilege! As a priest of the living God, you got to walk into the Holy of Holies and stand before the Ark of the Covenant. Zacharias was just doing his duty when an angel of the Lord appeared to him, standing at the right side of the altar of incense.

Here is a word for you if you desire to be used by God. Maybe you've told the Lord, "I want You to use me!" Perhaps you even feel called into full-time ministry.

That's great. Now get busy and do something.

"Well," you say, "I'm just waiting on the Lord."

But what does that mean? Is it relaxing in your La-Z-Boy at home, watching TV, and posting on Facebook? That is not how it will get done. You need to get yourself in motion and plunge your hands into the work somewhere. When God called Moses, what was he doing? He was tending his sheep. When David had an encounter with Goliath that changed his life, what had he been doing? Running an errand for his dad, delivering food to his older brothers who were out on the battle lines. God called Elisha when he was out plowing a field. Gideon was threshing wheat when

God's angel called him to deliver Israel from bondage to the Midianites. Peter and John were mending their nets with their dad when Jesus called them to be fishers of men.

In other words, they were doing something. They were in motion.

In my experience, it's much easier to steer a car when it's moving down the street than when it's parked in a garage.

Sometimes the way to find out what you are called to do for the Lord is by first finding out what you have *not* been called or equipped to do. As you roll up your sleeves to do kingdom work, you may find that what you had thought you were called to do hasn't been as productive as you might have hoped. But then as you are out and about, offering your services here and there, you may find that you have gifts you weren't even aware of.

Here is the key: be faithful in the little things.

And if you are faithful in those small areas of responsibility, God will open up greater opportunities for you. It was Warren Wiersbe who said, "You can never be too small for God to use, only too big." Just avail yourself to the Lord and watch what He will do.

I felt a call to ministry early in my life. I became a Christian at age seventeen. By age eighteen, I was already sure that I was called to serve God. I might have even imagined myself as some kind of preacher or evangelist. With those thoughts in mind, I made an appointment with Pastor Chuck Smith to talk it over. I went in, sat down in his office, and said, "Hi, Chuck. I'm Greg Laurie. I'm the one who draws this little *Living Water* cartoon tract." I handed him a tract, and he glanced at it and set it down on his desk.

"Okay," he said, "that's good."

"I want to serve God. I feel called to the ministry. I could lead a Bible study or something if you want me to."

Pastor Chuck said, "Greg, I want you to go meet with Pastor Romaine. He will tell you what to do."

Pastor Romaine? I didn't even know who Pastor Romaine was. But I quickly found out. Romaine was a former drill sergeant in the Marine Corps. After he had heard my little speech and glanced at my illustrated gospel tract, he pointed to the corner of the room.

"There is a broom," he said. "Pick it up and start sweeping over there. When you're done, go over to the bathrooms and clean the toilets. When you're done there, come back, and I'll give you something else to do."

Say what? I had thought they would ask me to preach! I thought they'd put me to work teaching Bible studies or—in view of my budding artistic talents—maybe designing and illustrating printed materials. But no, it seemed to me that they just wanted some free janitorial help.

I have since figured out, however, that they had something else in mind besides clean floors and toilets. This was a way to test me.

Did I really want to serve the Lord? Would I be faithful in the little things, doing them to the best of my ability for the glory of God? The truth is that if you can't be faithful in the small things, then you never will be faithful in the larger things.

Jesus said, "Whoever can be trusted with very little can also be trusted with much" (Luke 16:10, NIV). The bottom line, then, is that we need to do what is set before us to the best of our abilities and use the gifts that have been given to us, however and wherever we can.

But here is something to remember: The gifts of God don't come to us fully formed. Anyone with raw and undeveloped talents can strengthen those gifts of God through use and practice, application and discipline.

When I was a boy, I remember meeting a man who claimed to be an animator for Disney. It blew me away. Being a cartoonist at Disney Studios was the biggest dream of my life. But I wasn't sure about this guy.

I said to him, "Prove to me that you're an animator for Disney."

So he pulled out a pencil and drew a flawless Donald Duck. I was convinced—and in awe!

"How did you do that?" I asked.

Holding up his pencil, he said to me, "Greg, this is a magic pencil. If you will take this pencil and put it under your pillow and go to sleep, in the morning you will be able to draw like I do."

I don't know why, but I believed him—maybe because I had such a strong desire to be a real cartoonist. With my heart racing, I immediately ran out of the room and stuck that pencil under my pillow. In the morning, I grabbed the pencil and ran to find a piece of paper, drawing something on it the same way that I always had.

But there was no magic. Nothing had changed with my talents. As the years went by, however, and as I worked and practiced and spent countless hours with a pencil and paper, I began to develop my talents. The "magic" was in being faithful to use and perfect the gifts God had given me.

3. Zacharias and Elizabeth were godly people.

The text of Luke 1 says, "[Zacharias and Elizabeth] were both righteous before God, walking in all the commandments and ordinances of the Lord blameless" (verse 6). By the way, to be "blameless" doesn't mean they were sinless. It means they consistently followed God.

This couple was getting along in years and were well past the age of having children. Zacharias and Elizabeth had longed for a son and prayed for a son, but no child had come along. And now, seemingly, it was too late.

But it wasn't too late. In fact, God's program was right on time. In verse 13 the angel said to the old priest, "Do not be afraid,

Zacharias, for your prayer is heard; and your wife Elizabeth will bear you a son, and you shall call his name John." The original language seems to imply here that Zacharias had been praying for a son *in that very moment.* While he stood there before the altar of incense, representing the people, he might have been whispering in prayer, "Lord, I don't want to exploit this opportunity. But since I am standing in the Holy of Holies and You are already listening to me, please let me just throw in a quick prayer I've prayed many times before. Lord, please give us a son. I know we're old. I know we're past the age of parenthood. But Lord, I'm just going to ask You anyway. We long for a boy of our own."

Again, the implication of the language shows that God intended on answering that prayer in real time. Right there at that moment, Zacharias's prayer was heard in Heaven, and God sent an answer.

The same is true of your prayers. Your prayers are heard in Heaven.

"Well, Greg," someone will say to me, "my prayers really haven't been answered. God must not have heard me."

Are you sure of that? In Revelation 8:3 we read these words: "Another angel, having a golden censer, came and stood at the altar. He was given much incense, that he should offer it with the prayers of all the saints upon the golden altar which was before the throne."

God stores up all the prayers of His people. Every prayer that is ever prayed is recorded and stored. In fact, since God dwells in a timeless eternity, the prayer you prayed ten years ago is still before Him, just as much the prayer you prayed ten minutes ago.

God always answers our prayers; we just don't *like* the answers sometimes. He may answer yes or no or wait, but He will answer.

In this instance, the Lord was saying yes to Zacharias and Elizabeth after years and years of saying wait. In sending an angel to announce the answer to the priest's prayer, the Lord was saying, in effect, "I have noted your faithfulness. I have noted your humility. I have paid attention to the way you live."

Some people serve the Lord faithfully behind the scenes and imagine that no one really notices or cares. That isn't true; God notices and cares. And He promises that what we have done in secret for His name will someday be acknowledged openly.

In this passage, God was openly rewarding the faithfulness of Zacharias and Elizabeth and answering a prayer they had probably been repeating for more than thirty years. By that time, Zacharias may not have been praying with much enthusiasm or faith. It probably seemed to him that God hadn't really been listening. Then suddenly an angel came and told him that God had heard his prayer and was about to answer him with the deepest desire and longing of his heart.

And how did Zacharias react?

He reacted with doubt.

4. Zacharias was human and flawed, just like us.

In Luke 1:18 he replied to the angel, "How shall I know this? For I am an old man, and my wife is well advanced in years." In *The Message* paraphrase Zacharias said, "Do you expect me to believe this? I'm an old man and my wife is an old woman."

In reply the angel said, "I am Gabriel, who stands in the presence of God, and was sent to speak to you and bring you these glad tidings. But behold, you will be mute and not able to speak until the day these things take place, because you did not believe my words which will be fulfilled in their own time" (verses 19–20).

If he had exercised faith in that moment, Zacharias *could* have believed. Instead, he questioned and doubted. He wanted to believe, but he just wasn't sure. Gabriel replied, in effect, "Do you have any idea whom you're speaking to? I'm not your garden-variety angel. I stand in the presence of God Himself! I am Gabriel, a superangel with power and authority beyond your comprehension. And you are doubting my word?" As a consequence of this failure of Zacharias's faith, he suddenly became mute and couldn't speak a word.

The truth was that although God was answering this godly couple's heartfelt prayers, there were bigger things afoot than they realized at first. In fact, God was setting things in place to reveal His chosen and long-promised Messiah. Remember the verse I quoted earlier in the book? "But when the set time had fully come, God sent his Son, born of a woman, born under the law, to redeem those under the law, that we might receive adoption to sonship" (Galatians 4:4–5, NIV). God wasn't just giving Zacharias and Elizabeth a son; He was giving them the greatest prophet who ever lived—the very forerunner of the Messiah Himself.

Jesus said of John, "What did you go out into the wilderness to see? . . . A prophet? Yes, I say to you, and more than a prophet. For this is he of whom it is written: 'Behold, I send My messenger before Your face, who will prepare Your way before You.' Assuredly, I say to you, among those born of women there has not risen one greater than John the Baptist" (Matthew 11:7,9–11).

This means that John was greater than Abraham, Noah, Moses, Ezekiel, Isaiah, Jeremiah, Elijah, and Elisha. But what made him so great? Did John ever write a book of the Bible? No. Did John receive the commandments from God on Mount Sinai? No. Did God ever perform a miracle through John as He did through Elijah and Elisha? No.

Why, then, was John the greatest? Because John, and John alone, was the direct forerunner of Jesus Christ. *His greatness was a result of his closeness to Jesus,* and he was given the most wonderful privilege a person could ever receive: to announce that the Messiah was coming.

Unlike many prophets of the Lord, John was very popular in his own day and time. Josephus the historian actually wrote more about the life and ministry of John than he wrote about Jesus. To put it into the vernacular, John was a rock star in his culture. Everyone wanted to see John or be baptized by John. If there had been Fox News or CNN in his day, they would have been following him around with a camera. His words were the topic of conversation across the land, as he would blast the Pharisees and religious leaders with both barrels.

John had been set apart by God while he was still in his mother's womb. In Luke 1:15 we read, "For he will be great in the sight of the Lord, and shall drink neither wine nor strong drink. He will also be filled with the Holy Spirit, even from his mother's womb."

That's a significant verse when you're talking about the subject of abortion. There are those who say that an unborn child is nothing more than a glob of cells or a "potential human being." But how could a piece of tissue or a glob of cells be filled with the Holy Spirit? According to the Scriptures, a child in the womb is a *child*, a human person with an eternal soul.

A BOLD STATEMENT

Finally the day of John's birth arrived. When the couple's neighbors and friends gathered around to celebrate with them, they all speculated that the baby would be named Zacharias, after his dad. That's when Elizabeth spoke up (because Zacharias was mute and *couldn't* speak up) and told them all that the baby's name would be John.

John? Seriously?

When the relatives and friends heard this, they had a hard time believing it. "No one in your family has that name!" they objected. "Why would you name him that?" But when they brought Zacharias into the discussion, he took a tablet and wrote it down for them: "HIS NAME IS JOHN."

In the moment he affirmed that truth, the Lord miraculously opened Zacharias's mouth, activating the vocal chords that had been silent for so long, and he began to praise and glorify God. It was such a wonderful psalm of praise to the Lord that God had it recorded in the Scriptures for us, and we are able to read it (and join in) even today. Turning to his little infant son, perhaps holding him in his hands, Zacharias prophesied:

And you, child, will be called the prophet of the Highest;
For you will go before the face of the Lord to prepare His ways,

To give knowledge of salvation to His people

By the remission of their sins,

Through the tender mercy of our God,

With which the Dayspring from on high has visited us;

To give light to those who sit in darkness and the shadow
of death,

To guide our feet into the way of peace. (Luke 1:76–79)

WHAT DO WE LEARN FROM THIS PREQUEL?

From the lives of Zacharias, Elizabeth, and John, then, we learn that we should be humble, wait on the Lord, and serve Him right where we are. We also learn that we should keep praying and not give up, because our prayers are heard in Heaven. God takes note of them and will certainly answer them in His perfect time (and sometimes in totally unpredictable ways). We also should remember to believe what God tells us and act in faith rather than trusting our feelings or our own weak wisdom. And just as John was filled with the Holy Spirit from the womb, so we should submit to the daily filling of the Spirit, living our lives within His power and under His direction.

Sometimes when we look back at people in the pages of the Bible, we imagine them to be like stained glass images or think they walked around with halos over their heads. But that isn't true. There is only one perfect person who walked this earth, and that is Jesus. Everyone else was flawed. Mary and Joseph were flawed. Zacharias and Elizabeth were flawed. Even John the Baptist had his season of doubt late in life, when times were dark and he was discouraged in heart. Everyone—including people in the Bible—have their human weaknesses. It's important we understand that these were people just like us.

Again, Jesus said of John, "Among those born of women there is not a greater prophet than John the Baptist; but he who is least in the kingdom of God is greater than he" (Luke 7:28).

What? Greater than John? How could you and I ever be "greater" than him?

It's all about the covenants under which we live. John lived in the days of the Old Covenant, and we live in the days of the New Covenant. John (and everyone else in that day) approached God through a human high priest who would enter the Holy of Holies once a year. We can approach God through our High Priest, Jesus, at any time, any moment, 24/7.

Because of God's Son being born in a manger, living a perfect life, willingly going to the cross for our sins, and rising from the dead, life is radically different for those of us who have placed our faith in

Him and belong to Him. We actually can experience Jesus taking up residence inside of us, in the very center of our being.

John saw Jesus with his physical eyes on several occasions in his lifetime—but he didn't have Christ living within him. As Christians, we do.

The only thing better than that is to actually be with Christ in Heaven, and we have that to look forward to as well.

4

WHAT'S IN A NAME?

heard a story about a guy who got stuck with the last name of Odd. Can you imagine going through life with a name like that?

"So . . . your last name is Odd? That's odd."

"Hey, you're kind of *Odd*, aren't you?"

He just hated it. So after living with that miserable name his entire life, he actually gave instructions that, upon his death, nothing was to be written on his tombstone.

"Just leave it blank," he said, because he couldn't bear the thought of people walking through the cemetery, seeing his last name, and continuing to say, "That's odd."

Sure enough, honoring his wishes, they gave him a blank tombstone. A blank grave marker, however, is an unusual thing, and people walking through the cemetery would notice that featureless piece of granite. And they would say, "That's odd."

What's in a name? It all depends on what your name is. If you have gone through life with a name you didn't appreciate, you know that names can really make a difference. In the Old Testament, a man with the name of Jabez (which means "pain") made lemonade out of sour lemons. He used his name as a springboard to cry out to God for a special blessing, and the Lord answered his request (see 1 Chronicles 4:9–10).

Most people, however, don't have the determination or the faith of Jabez. One psychiatrist studied the names of fifteen thousand juvenile delinquents and discovered that those with odd or embarrassing names were in trouble four times as much as the others.

I had to go through life with the last name of Laurie—which is a girl's name, right? I would always—I mean, every time—be asked to spell it.

"What's your name?"

"Greg Laurie."

"*Laurie?*"

"Laurie."

"How do you spell it?"

"L-a-u-r-i-e."

"That's a girl's name."

"Yes, it is."

So maybe you, like me, went through life with a name you didn't like. Or maybe you got stuck with a nickname. I had the weirdest nickname of all: *Pogo.* So I was Pogo Laurie. (Don't you dare call me that, by the way. I will not answer to that.)

With the passing of time, certain names become popular. A couple of generations ago, names like Bob and Charles were popular. During the 1960s, many people rebelled against traditional names. I heard about a survey taken among those who lived in hippie communes. Here are some of the names they actually gave to their poor kids: Carrot, Sunshine, Fender, Gravy, and Doobie.

Can you imagine naming your kid Doobie?

The current trend is to find the coolest name, something of a designer name, for a baby—or perhaps a made-up name that no one has ever used before. Apparently, however, some of the more cautious parents are Googling the names they're thinking of giving to their kids. One parent said, "Nobody wants their baby's name to turn out to be a serial killer in Nebraska."

The top names for girls right now include Abigail, Emily, Madison, Chloe, Ava, Olivia, Isabella, and Sophia. The most popular names for boys are Logan, Lucas, Noah, Ethan, Jaden, Jacob, Liam, Mason, Jackson, and Aiden.

Then there are those weird parents who have interesting last names and think it's clever to give their child a funny first name to match (I'm not making these up): Chis B. Bacon, Eileen Dover, Gene Pool, Douglas Fir, Alba Tross, Anita Hug, Bea Clown, and Cookie Cutter.

In biblical days, however, names really meant something. Sometimes the name related to some physical attribute of the child at birth. For instance, in the book of Genesis we know that Isaac and Rebecca's firstborn was named Esau, which means "hairy." And why was he named Hairy? Because that is what he was when he came out of the womb. His twin brother came out after him, hanging on to Esau's heel. So they named this second boy Jacob, which means "heel catcher."

In the book of 1 Samuel, the wife of one of the priests gave birth to a baby in great distress when the news came that the Philistines had stolen the Ark of the Covenant. She named her baby Ichabod, meaning, "The glory has departed."

Can you imagine bringing a friend with that name home from school and introducing him to your mom?

"Hey Mom, this is my new friend, The Glory Has Departed."

But now we come to the most important name of all: the name that was given to our Lord when the angel Gabriel came to Mary and told her that she was going to bring forth a Son.

THE NAME ABOVE ALL NAMES

Do not be afraid, Mary, for you have found favor with God. And behold, you will conceive in your womb and bring forth a Son, and shall call His name JESUS. He will be great, and will be called the Son of the Highest; and the Lord

God will give Him the throne of His father David. And He will reign over the house of Jacob forever, and of His kingdom there will be no end. (Luke 1:30–33)

Jesus Christ is the name above all names. It is a name of great power.

If you don't believe me, just say it sometime—out loud. Say it in a crowded or even a noisy room. People might be all around you, talking like crazy. But when you say, "Jesus Christ" or "In the name of Jesus Christ," you'll be heard all over the room. People will turn to look. Conversations will stop.

The strange thing is, you could say, "Buddha" or "Hare Krishna" or even "Joseph Smith" and not create a ripple. But say the name of Jesus and something will happen in that room.

The Bible says that one day, at the name of Jesus Christ, every knee will bow and every tongue will confess that He is Lord, to the glory of God the Father (see Philippians 2:10–11).

In Isaiah 9:6-7, a great Christmas passage we have already quoted parts of in this book, we read a prophecy of the Lord's birth and of the names or titles He would be given:

For unto us a Child is born,
Unto us a Son is given;

And the government will be upon His shoulder.

And His name will be called

Wonderful, Counselor, Mighty God,

Everlasting Father, Prince of Peace.

Of the increase of His government and peace

There will be no end,

Upon the throne of David and over His kingdom.

As we noted earlier, Jesus Christ existed long before Bethlehem. As part of the Trinity, He has always existed and has no beginning or end. So the birth of our Lord was not when He began His existence. It merely was His entrance on to Planet Earth.

Each of the names or titles for Jesus recorded in the book of Isaiah gives us an insight not only into who He is, but also into the purpose of God for each one of us. Think of these names like five gifts under your tree that God has for you.

HIS NAME IS WONDERFUL

"His name will be called Wonderful." *This takes care of the dullness of life.*

The word *wonderful* comes from the root word *wonder.*

Bertrand Russell once claimed that at least half of the sins of mankind were caused by the fear of boredom.[1]

Probably the number one thing under most of our Christmas trees this year will be something electronic—an iPhone or an iPad or a Kindle or maybe a new digital camera. By the time this book is printed, there probably will be some new gadget on the market that didn't even exist when I started it. We have never had such advanced technology. Everywhere you go now, you see people with their eyes glued to their smartphones or tablets, checking out Facebook, reading e-mail, following Twitter, browsing Instagram, texting, or playing one of those addictive little games. And all the while you will hear people saying, "I am really bored."

The wonder quickly drains away from even the latest, most cutting-edge electronic devices. In fact, they will be outdated almost from the moment they leave the shelf. Just after you buy your new gadget, you'll hear chatter about a newer version with more megapixels or battery life or apps or whatever.

In fact, the gifts that we have under the tree are metaphors for life itself, saying, in effect, there is nothing this world has to offer that will fill the void in our lives. No matter what you have, no matter what you are able to buy, it will never satisfy you. (Or at least, not for very long.) An article I read quoted psychologist David Greenfield, who said, "Our culture is about distraction, numbing oneself. There is no self-reflection, no sitting still. It's absolutely exhausting."[2]

We need God in our lives! He is the only one who will satisfy the emptiness and the deep-down longing for something we can't even put words to. The Scriptures remind us to "be still, and know that [He is] God" (Psalm 46:10). *The Message* renders that verse, "Step out of the traffic! Take a long, loving look at me, your High God."

Despite all of the passing things of this world that will not last, there is Jesus, and He is *wonderful.* His very name is Wonder.

Every year at Christmas we open our gifts, and sometimes, frankly, we're a little disappointed. We wanted or expected one thing, only to receive something we didn't want or don't really care about. Or maybe we will be disappointed by the reactions of those to whom we've given gifts. We hoped our gifts would be hits, but oftentimes they are misses, and we will see that look of disappointment on their faces.

Life is full of letdowns isn't it? But God is never a letdown. God is wonderful.

We could take that word *wonder* apart and see elements of surprise, astonishment, admiration, bewilderment, worship, and awe. We used to say that God is awesome, but that word has lost some of its strength through overuse. What we really mean is that He inspires awe deep within us.

Our awesome God takes care of the dullness of our lives.

Medical science seeks to add years to your life, but only Jesus Christ can add life to your years and give you a life that is worth living. His name is Wonderful.

HIS NAME IS COUNSELOR

"His name will be called . . . Counselor." *This takes care of the decisions of life.*

Did you know that God Almighty wants to personally give you direction—that He has a plan custom-designed just for you?

I have read that during this time of the year, depression rates go up dramatically. More people check into hospitals. Suicide rates go up in the holiday season.

Think of all of the places where people look for answers today. Some go to the local bar and pour out their troubles to anyone who will listen. Some go to psychics or consult a horoscope for direction. Others will fork out money to go to "life coaches."

Still others will even go to Google trying to find answers, typing in, "What is the meaning of life?"

Help me, Google. Isn't that pitiful?

The current crop of iPhones have a feature called Siri, which acts like a personal assistant, reminding you of appointments or directing you to the closest coffee shop. Of course I have one because I'm into gadgets and love all the newest bells and whistles.

So the other day I asked Siri, "What is the meaning of life?"

Siri (who has a woman's voice) answered, "I don't know, but I think there is an app for that." I asked her again, and she replied, "All evidence to date suggests it is chocolate."

So I said, "Siri, why am I here?"

And my electronic assistant answered, "I don't know, and frankly I have been wondering that myself."

Listen, you don't need to go to Google or to Siri or to a psychic or to a psychologist for the answers of life. Everything you need to know about life and about God is found in the pages of your Bible. God will speak to you through His Word.

The Bible says of itself, "All Scripture is inspired by God and is useful to teach us what is true and to make us realize what is wrong in our lives. It corrects us when we are wrong and teaches us to do what is right. God uses it to prepare and equip his people to do every good work" (2 Timothy 3:16–17, NLT).

In Psalm 73 Asaph writes, "You guide me with your counsel, and afterward you will take me into glory" (verse 24, NIV). So in this life and in the next, you will find no better Counselor than your own Creator and Savior.

HIS NAME IS MIGHTY GOD

"His name will be called . . . Mighty God." *This takes care of the demands of life.*

Power is a big deal for men. Guys never can have too much power. If two men go to a gym, it's all about who can bench-press the most or do the most curls.

Or if it's a car, it's about how much horsepower you have. I have a friend who has a Shelby Mustang with 500 horsepower. He let me drive it once in a big, empty parking lot, and I admit that I coveted the car. With my friend riding shotgun, I put that baby into first gear, floored it, and we almost went airborne. Then I slammed it into second and threw it into third, and each time it felt like we left the ground. It was great fun!

Afterward he told me he was having more horsepower added to it. When I asked him why in the world he would do that, he smiled and said, "Bragging rights."

This sort of talk is even true among computer geeks. They're saying to each other, "How much RAM do you have in that thing? How much storage? How big is your hard drive?" It's always about power.

When you think about it, the history of mankind has been the story of acquiring, using, and abusing power. First it was manpower. Then it was horsepower, steam power, diesel power, and nuclear power. What we seem to lack is *willpower*.

The Mighty God, however, is present with us to give us all the power we need to live the Christian life.

Jesus wasn't a man who became God; that would be impossible. He was and is God who became a man. The all-powerful, eternal Creator and God became a baby, as difficult as that thought may be to wrap our minds around.

Max Lucado summed it up this way:

Divinity arrived. Heaven opened herself and placed her most precious one in a human womb.

The omnipotent, in one instant, made himself breakable. He who had been spirit became pierceable. He who was larger than the universe became an embryo. And he who sustains the world with a word chose to be dependent on the nourishment of a young girl. . . .

God had come near.[3]

That is what Christmas is all about. It's about the astounding, incomparable moment in human history when God became a man. Jesus was and is the mighty God, which takes care of all the demands of life. All the power that you will ever need to live the Christian life is available for you. As the apostle Peter wrote, "By his divine power, God has given us everything we need for living a godly life. We have received all of this by coming to know him, the one who called us to himself by means of his marvelous glory and excellence" (2 Peter 1:3, NLT).

Some people imagine that it must be really hard to be a Christian. I disagree with that assessment. Actually, it is *impossible* to be a Christian. It is absolutely beyond any of us apart from the help of the Holy Spirit. With His help, however, God will enable you to be the man or woman He has called you to be. As the Bible says, "With God all things are possible" (Matthew 19:26).

There will be many people opening electronic gizmos this Christmas only to find that their new toys don't work. So they will call the number for tech support and talk to someone on the phone (probably in India or Bangladesh). And those technicians are trained to always ask two questions before anything else. Question number one: Is the device plugged in? Question number two: Is the device turned on? You would be amazed at how many people's devices "don't work" because they're not plugged in or turned on.

God might ask the same of us. Are you plugged in? God will give you the power to live the life He has called you to live.

HIS NAME IS EVERLASTING FATHER

"His name will be called . . . Everlasting Father." *That takes care of the future of life.*

We know that life is more than what we are currently experiencing on Earth. In fact, the Bible teaches that you and I will live forever. That's a good thing, right?

Not necessarily.

It all depends on *where* you will live forever. You are an eternal soul. You are not a body that happens to have a soul; you are, as C. S. Lewis put it, a soul wrapped in a body. And the Bible teaches that one day your life on Earth will end, and if you're a believer in Jesus Christ, your soul and your resurrected body will go into God's presence in Heaven, where you will live with Him forever. But if you are not a believer, the Bible teaches that you will spend all eternity separated from God in a place called hell.

If you know the Everlasting Father, however, you don't have to be afraid of that.

Do you know Him in this way? Maybe you never got a chance to know your earthly father, which perhaps makes Christmas a difficult season for you. Maybe your dad walked out on the family, and you haven't seen him for years. Perhaps you were estranged from him at some point, and you have a very strange and strained relationship with him right now. You think of God being Father, and it's difficult for you to relate to.

I can understand that. I never had a father growing up and never knew who he was. I was basically conceived out of wedlock, and then my mom married and divorced seven different guys, and only one of them ever treated me like a son. He was the one who adopted me and gave me my last name, Laurie. So I had a love for that man, and later in life, I was able to go back and locate him and lead him to Christ.

When I came to Jesus Christ, it was so great to realize there was a Father in Heaven who always would be there for me, would never abandon me, would never desert me, and would always take time for me.

When my father who adopted me died, God was there. When my mother died, God was there. When my son died, God was there. He always will be there for me, and He always will be there for you because He is your Everlasting Father.

HIS NAME IS PRINCE OF PEACE

"His name will be called . . . Prince of Peace." *This takes care of the disturbances of life.*

In the storms of life, we long for peace. Life is filled with friction, hardship, and difficulty. There are troubled homes, troubled cities, and troubled people everywhere. But Jesus will be the Prince of Peace in your life. You won't find peace on a psychologist's couch, in a bottle, in a drug, in a human relationship, or in material possessions. You will find peace only in a relationship with God through Jesus Christ.

We remember the message the angels gave to the shepherds keeping watch over their flocks by night: "Glory to God in the highest, and on earth peace, goodwill toward men!" (Luke 2:14).

Yet when we look around our world at all the turmoil, strife, and anguish, we might find ourselves asking, "Where is it? Where is that peace?" Even the town of Bethlehem is frequently a very unsafe city, often at night. Where is the peace that the angels promised? Was it a joke? Were they mocking us?

No. That statement of the angels could better be translated, "Glory to God in the highest, and peace on earth *among men with whom God is well pleased.*"

You see, all of the problems we witness and experience in the world today are the result of humanity and its disobedience to God. Humanity itself has brought about the violence, unrest, turmoil, and war on the planet. But despite those things, you and I can have peace in the midst of the most troubled times and difficult situations.

Even when chaos rages all around, even in the middle of the storm, you can have peace because the Lord *is* your peace. In John 14, Jesus said, "I am leaving you with a gift—peace of mind and heart. And the peace I give is a gift the world cannot give. So don't be troubled or afraid" (verse 27, NLT).

Do you have this peace that Jesus spoke of? The Bible describes it as the peace that passes all human understanding. But before you can have the peace *of* God, you must first have peace *with* God, through Jesus Christ.

THE GOVERNMENT WILL BE ON HIS SHOULDER

Isaiah 9, verse 6, tells us, "And the Government will be upon His shoulder."

Yes, it *will* be. But it isn't yet.

There is a space of many years between "unto us a Child is born" and "the government will be upon His shoulder." We're still waiting for that latter statement to come to pass because we know the government is *not* on His shoulders yet. Trust me on that! When He is in charge of the government, it will run incomparably better than it runs now.

The day is coming, however, when He will rule and reign on Earth in righteousness. There will be no scandals. There will be no economic meltdowns. There will be no political shenanigans or grandstanding for the media. But that day is still coming; it is still future.

Before Jesus takes the government on His shoulder, He had to first take up something else on His shoulder: a cross. And that's just what He did: He took that cross and died on it.

We like to think of the sweet little baby in the manger and the singing angels and the visiting wise men and all of that—and all of those things are true. But if we miss why He came, we miss everything.

Before there was a planet called Earth, much less a garden called Eden or a city called Bethlehem, a decision was made in Heaven. And the decision was that Jesus would come to Earth and die for us.

So, what's in a name? It all depends on whose name it is. If it is the name of Jesus Christ, then everything you need is in that name. The Bible says, "Whoever calls on the name of the LORD shall be saved" (Acts 2:21).

His name is Wonderful.

5

CHRISTMAS, THE BIG ANNOUNCEMENT

I heard a story about a little girl who was coming home from Sunday school one morning and was very excited about the drawing she had done. Eagerly, she showed it to her mom.

"Mommy, look at the drawing I did in Sunday school of the Nativity scene. My teacher said it was the most unusual that she had ever seen."

As the mom looked at the drawing, she was immediately puzzled. It was obviously a picture of an airplane in flight. "Sweetheart," she said, "this is very good. But could you explain it to me? What is this airplane?"

A little indignant, her daughter replied, "That's the flight into Egypt."

"I see," her mom replied. "So . . . who is this mean-looking man in the cockpit?"

The little girl was exasperated. "Mom, that is Pontius the pilot!"

As she studied the drawing further, the girl's mom saw a little fat man seated behind Mary on the plane. She could not figure out who this could possibly be. Finally, she asked, "Honey, who is this fat man sitting behind Mary?"

The girl said, "Mom, that is round Jon Virgin!"

You remember, of course, that line from "Silent Night"? *Round yon virgin, mother and child.*

Truthfully, many people have difficulty with that part of the Christmas story. They stumble over the Bible's insistence that the Son of God Himself could be supernaturally conceived as a human being in the womb of the teenage virgin, Mary. How could such a thing be possible? Some mainline denominations have side-stepped that issue by simply denying that it ever happened.

But if you believe the Bible, there is only one possible answer to that question. Of course He was born of a virgin. No other conclusion is possible. And that is the birth we celebrate at this time of year.

AN UNLIKELY PLACE FOR A MIRACLE

In a seedy little town known for its sin and corruption, a teenage girl had a most unexpected visitor.

The mighty angel Gabriel, who no doubt could have taken on the whole Roman army single-handedly, appeared to Mary in the town of Nazareth. As surprising and awesome as his appearance must have surely been, his message to this girl was more amazing still. He told her that she was to have the privilege of being the mother of Israel's Messiah, who would be the Savior of the entire world.

In contrast to Zacharias, who initially doubted Gabriel's words, Mary believed at once. Here is how Dr. Luke, who gave years of his life to chronicle the life and times of Jesus, recorded that moment:

> Now in the sixth month the angel Gabriel was sent by God to a city of Galilee named Nazareth, to a virgin betrothed to a man whose name was Joseph, of the house of David. The virgin's name was Mary. And having come in, the angel said to her, "Rejoice, highly favored one, the Lord is with you; blessed are you among women!"
>
> But when she saw him, she was troubled at his saying, and considered what manner of greeting this was. Then the angel said to her, "Do not be afraid, Mary, for you have found favor with God. And behold, you will conceive in your womb and bring forth a Son, and shall call His name JESUS. He will be great, and will be called the Son of the Highest; and the Lord God will give Him the throne of His father David. And He will reign over the house of Jacob forever, and of His kingdom there will be no end."
>
> Then Mary said to the angel, "How can this be, since I do not know a man?"

And the angel answered and said to her, "The Holy Spirit will come upon you, and the power of the Highest will overshadow you; therefore, also, that Holy One who is to be born will be called the Son of God. Now indeed, Elizabeth your relative has also conceived a son in her old age; and this is now the sixth month for her who was called barren. For with God nothing will be impossible."

Then Mary said, "Behold the maidservant of the Lord! Let it be to me according to your word." And the angel departed from her. (Luke 1:26–38)

Let's take a closer look at this amazing story in all of its simplicity and glory. Here are a few points to consider.

MARY LIVED A GODLY LIFE IN AN UNGODLY PLACE

This was not the first time a holy angel from Heaven was dispatched to a godless city. In the book of Genesis, angels were sent into Sodom to deliver Lot and his family from the destruction that was coming. Sodom and Gomorrah were known as wicked cities in their day, and Nazareth also was known for its sin.

Have you noticed how some cities have certain nicknames? Rome is called the Eternal City. Paris is called the City of Light. New

York is known as "the city that never sleeps." And Vegas? Well, "What happens in Vegas stays in Vegas." (But of course, it really doesn't.) Nazareth, in the first century, could have been called Sin City, overrun as it was with Roman soldiers.

Nazareth was one of those towns you went through to get to somewhere else. It definitely was not a destination resort. One commentator described it as "a hotbed of corruption." This explains why Nathanael, upon hearing that Jesus came from Nazareth, responded in surprise, "Can anything good come out of Nazareth?" (John 1:46).

Let's imagine that Jesus was born on Earth today instead of more than two thousand years ago. Where would you expect Him to be born? Jerusalem? Maybe in Rome or London or Paris? How about New York City, Boston, or Los Angeles? What if you heard that Jesus had entered this world in Plain City, Utah? That is an actual place. Or what if the Messiah had grown up in Frog Eye, Alabama, or Bald Knob, Arkansas? What would it have been like if He had lived most of His years in San Francisco or Las Vegas? *The Savior has arrived! Jesus of Las Vegas!*

Do you see how it changes the way you view it? That's what it would have been like for people in much of Israel to hear about "Jesus of Nazareth."

Nevertheless, that is where Mary lived and most likely where she had grown up. She was Mary of Nazareth. Here was a young woman with royal blood in her veins, a lineage that went back to King David, and she lived in a corrupt, sinful city. She was like a lily poking up through a manure pile. Living in an impure environment, she stayed pure. Mary showed that it is possible to live a holy life in an unholy place.

In chapter 2 of his second letter, the apostle Peter described the influence of the world on two prominent Old Testament believers: the first was Noah and the second was Lot.

Noah lived an uncompromised life at a place and time where "every inclination of the thoughts of the human heart was only evil all the time" (Genesis 6:5, NIV). But "Noah found favor in the eyes of the LORD. . . . Noah was a righteous man, blameless among the people of his time, and he walked faithfully with God" (verses 8–9, NIV). The world at that time was like an overflowing septic tank. Yet Noah faithfully served the Lord in the midst of that godless, cynical culture. He raised his family as believers, he preached to others, and he maintained a walk of integrity and a close personal relationship with God.

The second man Peter mentioned was Lot, Abraham's nephew, who ended up living with his family in the utterly corrupt city of

Sodom. Interestingly, the Bible tells us that although Lot lived in that wicked place, he wasn't comfortable with it. He didn't like it. Peter wrote, "But God also rescued Lot out of Sodom because he was a righteous man who was sick of the shameful immorality of the wicked people around him. Yes, Lot was a righteous man who was tormented in his soul by the wickedness he saw and heard day after day" (2 Peter 2:7–8, NLT).

But even though Lot knew he ought to get his family out of that evil place, he hesitated and was reluctant to leave. Finally God sent a couple of angels to take Lot, his wife, and their two daughters by the hands and effectively drag them out of the city. When it came right down to it, they didn't want to go. It was like pulling a kid out of a candy store. Tragically, Lot's testimony had become so weak and ineffective that when he tried to warn his sons-in-law about God's approaching judgment, they laughed right in his face.

There is no power in a compromised life. Compromised people reach no one. Lot eventually escaped the destruction of Sodom and Gomorrah, but his family was ruined in the process.

Here is the question for each of us as we consider the lives of Mary in Nazareth, Noah in a wicked and violent world, and Lot in a corrupt city: *Are you changing your culture, or is your culture changing you?* Are you a thermometer or a thermostat? A thermometer is affected by its surroundings as its mercury goes up or down according to the temperature. A thermostat, however, changes the temperature of a room. Which are you? Do you merely react to what is happening around you, or are you actually making an impact on your surroundings?

Lot was a thermometer. He may not have liked the temperature, but he couldn't or wouldn't do anything about it. Noah and Mary were thermostats and stood in contrast to their cultures. You and I may sometimes blame our wicked culture for the way we are, but in reality, it is our task as followers of Jesus Christ to permeate and affect our culture.

When a Christian walks into a room, he or she should change the atmosphere. In some sense, people in the room should be aware that a follower of Christ has just come through the door. It should affect the conversation. I don't mean that you should come across as overly pious or self-righteous, looking down your nose at people. But if you are walking with Jesus Christ and are filled with His Spirit, then you definitely will bring His Presence into whatever room you enter.

Mary was a godly young woman living in an ungodly place. How young was she? Commentators say she may have been as young as twelve and probably was no older than fourteen. Had she been like many other teens of her time, she might have married a poor man, gave birth to numerous poor children, never traveled more than a few miles from her home, and died without the world ever knowing her name. Nevertheless, God chose her, and that made all the difference in her life. Even though she was a nobody living in a nothing town in the middle of nowhere, God said, in effect, "This is the woman I choose for the highest honor of all."

This is a good reminder to us that God uses nobodies to tell everybody about Somebody. God can use you where you are, *wherever* you are.

Mary was handpicked to fulfill a landmark Old Testament prophecy: "Therefore the Lord Himself will give you a sign: Behold, the virgin shall conceive and bear a Son, and shall call His name Immanuel" (Isaiah 7:14).

As a good Jewish girl, Mary would have known this Scripture passage from her earliest days. I would imagine that in her wildest dreams, she never would have thought she would be the one actually spoken of in this prophecy. *Who, me? I'm going to be the mother of the Messiah? I'm going to carry the Son of God in my womb?* When that truth finally dawned on her, it must have blown her away.

We read in Luke 1:28, "Having come in, the angel said to her,

'Rejoice, highly favored one, the Lord is with you; blessed are you among women!' " The phrase *come in* implies that Mary was in the house alone. She probably was doing the domestic chores of a twelve- to thirteen-year-old Jewish girl.

In the King James Version, Gabriel says, "Hail. . . ." That does not mean he was offering worship or praise to her. It was simply old English for "Hi" or "Hello."

In Hawaii they say, "How's it, brah?"

If you live in Australia, you say, "G'day."

If you're from New York or Philadelphia, you say, "Yo!"

In other words, it was just a simple greeting, and we shouldn't read anything else into it. Suddenly, an immensely powerful angel was standing in a humble little house in Nazareth, saying, "Hey, Mary. Good morning. You are a very privileged girl. God has extended His hand of grace to you."

And she would need that grace!

In fact, Mary was startled by that appearance and that greeting, just as you or I would have been. One Bible version says, "She was thoroughly shaken, wondering what was behind a greeting like that" (Luke 1:29, MSG).

As we have noted, seeing any angel of God would drop most of us to our knees, and Gabriel was no ordinary angel—not by a long shot!

FIVE QUICK FACTS ABOUT THE MESSENGER

1. Gabriel is mentioned in both the Old and New Testaments.

This mighty angel's first appearance is in the book of Daniel, where he spoke to the prophet about the coming Messiah. It seems that Gabriel's ministry is specifically tied to telling people about Jesus. When he appeared to Daniel, he came with a greeting that was something similar to what he said to Mary. In Daniel 9:23 Gabriel said, "I have come to tell you, for you are greatly beloved."

2. Gabriel stands in the presence of the Lord.

This is how he described himself when he came to Zacharias, who would be the father of John the Baptist. When the old man expressed doubt about the angel's words, Gabriel replied, "I am Gabriel. I stand in the presence of God" (Luke 1:19, NIV). In other words, this powerful being has immediate access to the Almighty Himself.

3. Gabriel is one of two angels mentioned by name in the Bible.

The other angel named in the Bible is Michael the archangel. Is Gabriel an archangel, too? The Bible doesn't say. Clearly, he is (to this day) a high-ranking angel. Lucifer, the "son of the morning"

(Isaiah 14:12), also was once a holy, powerful angel, but he lost his place of privilege when he fell and became Satan, or the Devil.

4. Gabriel looks like a man.

In fact, the name *Gabriel* means "man of God." In Daniel's second encounter with Gabriel, the prophet described him as a man. All of this to say . . . there are no female angels in the Bible. In spite of this fact, however, we usually use the term *angel* in a feminine way. We will say, "She's an angel." When we see angels portrayed in paintings or cartoons, they're often depicted as being women. I know that it's a disappointment, but "chick angels" don't exist—at least in the Bible. Angels always appear as men.

5. Gabriel scares people because he is so awesome and powerful.

His first words to Zacharias were, "Do not be afraid." The prophet Daniel relates an encounter with Gabriel by saying, "He came up to me, but when he got close I became terrified and fell facedown on the ground" (Daniel 8:17, MSG). In the Luke passage, we read that Mary "was troubled at his saying, and considered what manner of greeting this was" (1:29).

Was it the angel's appearance or his message that left her so stunned? Have you ever received a message that left you absolutely stunned? Maybe it was good news, and maybe it was bad news, but for a few seconds you couldn't speak or move. That was the case with Mary in her little home in Nazareth.

MARY WAS SURPRISED AT HER SELECTION

Mary was honestly surprised that God had selected her and not someone else. There was no sense of "I deserve this recognition" or "It's about time! I've earned this!" No, she was completely overwhelmed that the Lord would confer such a privilege on someone like her.

That's the way it is with godly people. When people are truly close to the Lord, you won't hear them boasting about their devotion or trying to draw attention to themselves. You won't hear them talking about what they have done for God. They always will speak of what God has done for them—how kind, merciful, and gracious God has been to them.

This is why John, in his gospel, describes himself as the disciple whom Jesus loved. Does that sound a little self-serving, like John was bragging about being someone Jesus was especially attached to? Not really. And isn't it better than saying, "I am the disciple who loved Jesus"? John was showing his humility with these words. He was saying, "My love is fickle. My love can vary with the circumstances.

But the love of Jesus is constant and never changes. He loves me, and He always will!"

John boasts about God's love for him rather than about his love for God. By the way, this is also the mark of a good testimony, your story of how you came to Christ. Such a testimony always will focus on what Christ gave up to save you, not on what you gave up to follow Him. I've heard people's testimonies that make it sound as though their past was more interesting than their present and future. They will say things like, "Well, I used to party and have lots of fun doing wild and crazy things. Then I heard about Jesus and took up the old rugged cross. Now I just read my Bible all day. One day I'll die and go to Heaven, where I will float around and play a harp."

Really?

Who will be drawn to Christ by words like those? Don't focus on the past you walked away from. Focus instead on the life God has given you today and what He has promised concerning your future. Focus on what God has done for you.

Though Mary was a virtuous woman and a godly woman, she was not a sinless woman. Mary was a sinner just like us. Was she privileged, set apart, and called by God? Yes! But she also was a sinful, fallen human being. In her beautiful song of praise in Luke, chapter 1, she began by saying, "My soul magnifies the Lord, and my spirit has rejoiced in God my Savior" (verses 46-47).

Even Mary needed a Savior. Perhaps that was part of her surprise in being selected for such an unbelievable task and privilege. She may not have felt worthy for an honor like that. But who would?

In Luke 1:31–33, Gabriel went on to describe the Child whom Mary would bear:

> And behold, you will conceive in your womb and bring forth a Son, and shall call His name JESUS. He will be great, and will be called the Son of the Highest; and the Lord God will give Him the throne of His father David. And He will reign over the house of Jacob forever, and of His kingdom there will be no end.

At that time, Jesus was a common name. Many young boys of that era were named Jesus. In Hebrew it's the name *Joshua*, which means "Jehovah is salvation." But of all the boys and men who were ever called Jesus or Joshua, only one could embody the full meaning of that name, and that is Jesus the Christ.

Gabriel said, "He will be great." The word *great* in the original language comes from the root word *megas*, from which we draw our English term *mega*. We use it in words like megaphone, megachurch, and megastore. It conveys the idea of bigness or greatness, and if ever that word applied to anyone, it applies to

Jesus. He is great and the very definition of the word great. Today people in our culture may belittle His name, scoff at His name, slander His name, or drag His name through the mud. But one day every knee in the universe will bow before that name, acknowledging Him as King of kings and Lord of lords.

Also notice that in verse 32, Gabriel says that God "will give Him the throne of His father David." I find that fascinating. David is such a unique figure in the Scriptures. He is described on one hand as "the sweet psalmist of Israel" (2 Samuel 23:1) and "a man after [God's] own heart" (1 Samuel 13:14). But we also know of his foibles, shortcomings, and sins.

Two other names connected to David serve well to sum up his whole life: (1) Goliath and (2) Bathsheba. In Goliath we recall David's greatest victory, defeating a nine-foot-six-inch Philistine warrior with only a sling and a stone. With Bathsheba, David suffered his most profound defeat, as he pursued a married woman and had an affair with her that resulted in the murder of her husband—who happened to be one of David's most loyal soldiers.

David was a flawed man, and yet Jesus was called "the Root and the Offspring of David" and the "Son of David." In spite of David's failings, the Lord allowed Himself to be intimately connected with him.

As I stated in an earlier chapter, if you imagine that you have a dysfunctional family, then take a look at Jesus' family tree!

I was talking to my friend Bob Shank the other day about family trees, and he made this observation: "Someone warned me about not examining the Shank family tree too closely because I might find a few Shanks hanging from that tree!"

It's true for most of us. We may want to go back and look into our ancestors and our heritage, but we might not like all that we find there. We all want to think we are connected to royalty or some great American historical figure, but we might also unearth a few swindlers and a murderer or two.

It's the same in the Lord's family tree. There are some unsavory characters who made it into the most exclusive genealogy in human history, including prostitutes, liars, cheats, adulterers, and even a murderer.

What does this say to us?

It all points to one thing: Christ came into the world to save sinners. He Himself was sinless, but He was born into a long family line of flawed, sinful, broken people. David committed some terrible sins, yet throughout the ministry of Christ, He was known as "the Son of David."

"HOW WILL THIS BE?"

Mary's question to Gabriel was both natural and appropriate. In Luke 1: 34 she said, "How will this be,. . . since I am a virgin?" (NIV).

This is a different question altogether from the doubting response Zacharias gave to the angel. When Gabriel told the old priest that he and Elizabeth were going to have a son, his response was more like, "No, I don't think so. She's too old and so am I. It's not going to happen."

Mary, however, wasn't disbelieving. She was more interested in how God was going to pull this off, as she was a virgin and had never known a man. Gabriel wasn't offended by the question at all, and he gave her this beautiful reply: "The Holy Spirit will come upon you, and the power of the Highest will overshadow you; therefore, also, that Holy One who is to be born will be called the Son of God" (Luke 1:35).

We don't know how this actually happened or how long it took for this amazing event to transpire. But we can sum it up by saying that Mary's womb became the Holy of Holies for the Son of God.

As a man, I'm not sure that I understand this at all. But women who have been mothers know what it's like to carry a child in their womb. There is a connection between mother and child that a father can never fully know. But just imagine not only carrying a child within you, but also understanding that this baby was God incarnate.

Incredible? Incomprehensible? Perhaps. But completely true.

MARY WAS COMPLETELY OBEDIENT

Mary answered the angel, "Behold the maidservant of the Lord! Let it be to me according to your word" (Luke 1:38).

Have you ever said something similar to God?

"Lord, let it be to me according to Your word."

Even though Mary didn't begin to understand everything these developments meant for her, she was fully obedient and submissive to the Lord. This is the kind of attitude that God looks for in His servants: a childlike faith and obedience.

Since they were very little, my grandchildren have been fully willing to jump into my arms. If I ask them to jump, they will jump. I remember when little Christopher was just over a year old. He couldn't even talk yet, but he understood about jumping. I would say, "Okay, Christopher. Ready? One, two, three, *jump.*" And he would just let himself fall. If I hadn't been there to catch him, there would have been trouble. But I was always there to catch him, and he knew that. He completely depended on my being there for him. It was and is a complete acceptance that I love him and won't let any harm come to him.

But what's our response when God says, "Jump"?

Do we fall into His arms, or do we hesitate and hold back? Do we leap into the dark, or do we say, "I'm afraid! What if You drop me?"

And God replies, "I won't drop you. Jump! Come on, just go for it. I will be with you."

That's what Mary did. When God said "jump," she simply fell into His strong arms. As Corrie ten Boom has said, "Never be afraid to trust an unknown future to a known God."

Many times you and I will wonder about the will of God for our lives. Let me suggest this: *Obedience to revealed truth guarantees guidance in matters unrevealed.* The wind of God is always blowing, but you need to hoist your sail. I would suggest that you simply say, "Lord, I'm willing to obey, even though I don't completely understand what it is You're asking me to do."

In Romans 12:1–2, the apostle Paul gives us clear directions for how to know God's will:

> Therefore, I urge you, brothers and sisters, in view of God's mercy, to offer your bodies as a living sacrifice, holy and pleasing to God—this is your true and proper worship. Do not conform to the pattern of this world, but be transformed by the renewing of your mind. Then you will be able to test and approve what God's will is—his good, pleasing and perfect will. (NIV)

Notice the passage starts out with offering yourself to God.

It doesn't say to find out God's will first and then determine if you want to obey it. It says to commit yourself to the Lord. Present yourself as a living sacrifice—and don't let yourself be transformed by the world. Another translation puts it like this: "Don't let the world around you squeeze you into its own mould, but let God re-mould your minds from within, so that you may prove in practice that the plan of God for you is good, meets all his demands and moves towards the goal of true maturity" (PH).

First commit yourself unreservedly to Him, and He will show you His will.

That's what Mary did. After the angel told her how her whole life would change forever, she said, "Behold the maidservant of the Lord! Let it be to me according to your word."

Even so, her head must have been swimming. Uppermost in her mind must have been, *How am I going to explain this to Joseph? When I tell him what really happened, he will never buy it!* "Um, *Joseph, . . . I'm pregnant, but it's not what you think. Listen, Joseph. An angel came and spoke to me. It turns out that I am the virgin spoken of in the book of Isaiah. I haven't been unfaithful; I have been chosen by God!*"

At first Joseph didn't buy it. But God already had that base covered and spoke to Joseph Himself.

THE UNSUNG HERO

Joseph doesn't get nearly the credit he deserves in the Christmas story. Matthew 1:19 assures us that he was a righteous man. No doubt he was deeply in love with Mary, his young bride-to-be, and was severely jolted by the news that she was with child. They were engaged at the time, which in that culture was like being married.

In the Hebrew culture of that day, you didn't get to decide whom you would marry, as we do today. Your parents decided, and that was that. Sometimes the two sets of parents would espouse a son to a daughter while the children were still little. At eight years old, you might already know who your wife or husband would be. Once you entered into the twelve-month engagement, or espousal period, it was like being married already, although the man and woman would live in separate houses, and there were no sexual relations involved at that point. The wedding ceremony would come at the end of the twelve months. This was the period in which Mary became pregnant, and her supposed offense was equivalent to being unfaithful after marriage.

Even so, Joseph loved this girl and probably was at his wit's end, not knowing what to do about it. He didn't want to see her publicly shamed or put to death. Finally he concluded in his heart, "I'm going to have to put her away. I'm going to have to end our marriage—and do it as quietly as possible."

Joseph is really a hero in this story. No, there are very few songs about him, and if he went missing from our Nativity sets, we might not even notice. And yet Joseph was chosen for his role as surely as Mary was for hers. God the Father in Heaven chose Joseph to be a stepfather or father figure on Earth for Jesus.

You would have thought that God would have selected a priest for that honor. But no, He chose a blue-collar guy, a hard-working carpenter. And it was no mistake that Jesus grew up in a carpenter's home. Carpenters create new things and fix broken things, and these skills became part of Jesus' heritage. No doubt Joseph taught Jesus how to put His back into a task, how to be responsible, and how to put in a hard day's work.

The greatest crisis in Joseph's life, however, had to be those moments when Mary told him of her pregnancy, and he was wrestling in his mind and heart, trying to figure out what in the world he should do. One night he fell asleep pondering these things and had an angelic encounter of his own. In Matthew 1:20–21 we read, "But while he thought about these things, behold, an angel of the Lord appeared to him in a dream, saying, 'Joseph, son of David, do not be afraid to take to you Mary your wife, for that which is conceived in her is of the Holy Spirit. And she will bring forth a Son, and you shall call His name Jesus, for He will save His people from their sins.' "

That was all Joseph needed to hear. He was on board with Mary and Jesus for the rest of his life.

It might not have been that way with someone else. A lesser man might have walked away, even after learning the truth. Do you imagine that other carpenters at the work site would have accepted the story of a virgin birth? Not a chance! Can you imagine Joseph showing up at work with his lunch box, noticing the glances of his fellow workmen, and hearing their whispered comments?

He knew he would be laughed at. He knew they would never believe the truth.

But Joseph squared his shoulders, set his jaw, and endured it all for the sake of his beloved Mary and her little son Jesus.

It was as though Mary had to go through life with a scarlet *A* (for adulteress) sewn on the front of her garment. Though she was pure and had lived a clean and devoted life, Mary had to go through her years with the reputation of a loose woman. Later in the Lord's ministry, some Pharisees threw the old rumors back in His face. They said, "We aren't illegitimate children! God himself is our true Father" (John 8:41, NLT).

This was equivalent to saying to Jesus, "Well, at least we weren't conceived out of wedlock like *You*." But of course Jesus was not conceived out of wedlock or born of fornication. He was supernaturally conceived in Mary's womb. Even so, Joseph and Mary had to go through life with this false slander, with all the attendant whispers and glances continually thrown in their faces. It was part of the price they paid for the great privilege that had come to them.

The fact is that when God blesses a person, there is a price to pay.

When God uses a person, there is a sacrifice to be made.

When you say (and mean it with all your heart), "Let it be to me according to Your Word," don't imagine that it will put you on an easy path. It probably won't be easy at all, but it could be very, very fruitful. Later in life when you look back, you won't regret it.

THE VIRGIN BIRTH IS NONNEGOTIABLE

How important is it to hold to and believe in the virgin birth of Jesus? Some would say, "You really don't need to believe in the virgin birth of Jesus to be a Christian. You need to simply believe in His death and resurrection."

And yet, of what *value* are the death and resurrection of Jesus if He wasn't supernaturally conceived? Because of the manner of this conception, Christ did not inherit a sinful nature. He was the sinless Son of God who became "the Lamb of God who takes away the sin of the world" (John 1:29). As the apostle Paul wrote, "God made him who had no sin to be sin for us, so that in him we might become the righteousness of God" (2 Corinthians 5:21, NIV).

If you doubt the virgin birth, then you really have to doubt whether Christ could die for your sins and reconcile you with God. Without the virgin birth, there is no sinless Christ. Without a sinless Christ, there is no atonement. Without atonement, there is no forgiveness. Without forgiveness, there is no hope of Heaven. Without a hope of Heaven, there is really no hope at all in life. We might as well just live for today and selfishly grab all the pleasure that we can.

If you doubt the virgin birth, then you have to doubt the truthfulness of God's Word, because it plainly says that Jesus was born of a virgin.

If you doubt the virgin birth, then you have to question the character of Mary. If her conception wasn't supernatural, then she was immoral, and Jesus was born out of wedlock.

If you doubt the virgin birth, then you can't put any confidence in Christ Himself, because He is a mere man and no Savior at all.

In fact, the virgin birth is central to everything we believe.

Jesus was supernaturally conceived in Mary's womb, lived a perfect life, and died a horrific death on the cross, giving Himself for the sins of the world and then rising again after three days in the tomb.

As hard as it may be to wrap our minds around this truth, Jesus was born to die. The shadow of the cross hung over Him even in the cradle. When He was a little older, the Magi from the East came to visit Him, bringing Him gifts of gold, frankincense, and myrrh. That last gift, myrrh, was an embalming element. It would be like giving someone a jar of formaldehyde as a birthday present. Why would the wise men give the Christ child such a gift? Because they had insight into the fact that He had been born to die for the sins of humanity.

Looking into the eyes of an amazed and wondering Mary and Joseph in the temple, the old man Simeon held the infant Jesus in his arms and said, "This child is destined to cause the falling and rising of many in Israel, and to be a sign that will be spoken against, so that the thoughts of many hearts will be revealed. And a sword will pierce your own soul too" (Luke 2:34–35, NIV).

Jesus had come on a rescue mission from Heaven to save us all from our sins.

"You can take joy in that," Simeon seemed to say, looking at Mary, "but He will pay a great price . . . and so will you."

PART TWO

CHRISTMAS, LOST AND FOUND

6

DON'T MISS CHRISTMAS

O n December 17, 1903, brothers Orville and Wilbur Wright made the first successful powered airplane flight near Kitty Hawk, North Carolina. With Orville at the controls, the primitive aircraft got off the ground for twelve seconds.

Wilbur rushed to the telegraph office in Kitty Hawk to send a message to their family in Ohio about what they had accomplished that day. The message read,

> Success four flights thursday [*sic*] morning all against twenty one mile wind started from Level with engine power alone average speed through air thirty one miles . . . inform Press home Christmas.[1]

Upon receiving the telegram, their father prepared a message for the press, describing what the brothers pulled off and mentioning that Orville and Wilbur would be home for Christmas. A number of days later, the newspaper ran a brief story saying the Wright brothers would be home for Christmas.[2]

Talk about missing the point! Here was the most important story of the year—indeed of the century—about man's first airplane flight, and the press missed it. It blew right over their heads.

That's exactly how Christmas is for many today.

MISSING THE POINT

So many people completely miss the point of Christmas. The truth is, Christmas has been hijacked by secular culture and emptied of its meaning. And there is so much fantasy and myth imposed on this holiday that people have become numb to the real miracle of Christ's birth.

I heard the story of a woman who took her little boy to Sunday school for the first time, where he heard the story of our Lord's birth. He'd never heard anything like it. When he got home, he excitedly described it all to his mom.

"Mom," he said, "today I learned about the very first Christmas in Sunday school. There wasn't a Santa Claus back then, but there were these three skinny guys on camels that had to deliver all of the toys. And Rudolph the Red-Nosed Reindeer with his nose so bright wasn't there yet, so they had to have this big spotlight from the sky to guide these three skinny guys around."

That's a pretty good illustration of how our reference point has changed as a culture. Many of our children start with the shallow Christmas myths but don't know anything about the real, historical account that launched everything—the greatest story of all.

In all the madness that accompanies this season, we can actually miss Christmas.

You say, "Greg, it's not possible to miss Christmas. My Sunday newspaper weighs in at about thirty pounds because it is stuffed with ads pressuring me to buy stuff. The TV is reminding me. The radio is reminding me. Even when I go on the Internet, there are those obnoxious little pop-up ads that remind me. To tell you the truth, I'm worn out by it all."

I'm reminded of a story I heard about a mother who was running furiously from store to store on Christmas Eve to get those last-minute gifts. Suddenly she realized that she had lost track of her little three-year-old son. In a panic, she retraced her steps and found her little guy with his nose pressed up against a frosty window, gazing at a manger scene.

When he heard his mother shout out his name, he said, "Mommy, Mommy, look! It's the baby Jesus in the hay."

The stressed-out mom grabbed him and jerked him away, saying, "We don't have time for that. Can't you see that Mommy is trying to get ready for Christmas?"

That is how it can be. Because of all the clutter of Xmas—and

I use that term intentionally—we forget about the Christ of Christmas. So come back to the manger of Bethlehem, and Christmas will come alive to you.

WHO'S RESPONSIBLE FOR THIS?

A woman was doing some last-minute Christmas shopping at a crowded mall. She was tired of fighting the crowds and standing in lines and getting all those gifts and so forth. Finally almost done with her shopping, she pushed the elevator button, the door opened, and it was packed with people.

Have you ever had that moment? Everyone looks at you with an expression that says, "Don't come in here." But you really don't want to wait any longer because you've already waited a long time.

So the exhausted woman wedged her way into the packed elevator. As they were on their way down, she just couldn't hold in her frustrations any longer. Breaking all the rules of elevator decorum, she suddenly blurted out, "Whoever is responsible for this whole Christmas thing ought to be arrested, strung up, and shot!" A few others nodded in agreement.

And then, from the back of the elevator, came a single voice that said, "Don't worry. They already crucified Him."

Now Jesus is certainly not responsible for the madness of Christmas. He wasn't born that we might shop; He was born to die that we might live. There was no room for Him at the inn. In fact, it seems the only place where there was room for Him was on the cross.

But here is the irony: Often those who are conversant with spiritual truth are in the greatest danger of indifference. If you are in a good, Bible-teaching church, you are blessed with the privilege of hearing the Word of God taught day and in and day out. But there is a danger that comes with that blessing. If you listen to those truths with a wrong heart, with no intention of applying what you've heard, if you're just going through the motions, your heart can actually grow hard toward the things of God.

If contact with holy things does not convert or change your heart, it can cause your heart to become jaded and cynical. We can become indifferent or flippant about the tender story of the Nativity. We can become jaded to the message of the gospel because we have heard it so many times. As so many through the years have affirmed, familiarity breeds contempt.

Don't let that happen to you. Keep a tender and an open heart toward God. Don't let religion crowd out Jesus.

Don't miss Christmas.

Make time for Jesus. Make room for Jesus. I love the Christmas hymn "Joy to the World" because one of the lines says, "Let every heart prepare Him room."

Make room for Him this year.

IN HONOR OF THE KING

Maybe you've heard the story about the man who went to a garage sale, where he noticed something under a tarp in the back of the garage. Pulling the tarp back, he saw that it was an old, classic Harley Davidson motorcycle.

The bike didn't seem to be part of the sale, but the man thought that it wouldn't do any harm to ask about it.

"Say," he said to the owner, "do you want to sell that thing?"

The homeowner thought for a moment and then shrugged his shoulders. "You know," he said, "I've been meaning to get it fixed up. But I don't think I'll ever get around to it. So I might as well sell it."

"How much do you want for it?"

"Well, if I took it down to the junkyard, they'd probably give me thirty-five bucks for it. So just give me the thirty-five bucks and you can take it."

So they agreed, and Bob, the man who was buying the motorcycle, loaded it up in his truck and took it home. For several months he let the old bike sit in his own garage, under a tarp, just like the previous owner had. But then he said to himself, *I need a project. I'm going to put this old Harley back together.*

Getting ready for his project, Bob called the local Harley dealer to check on a few major parts he would need to restore the bike.

The Harley guy asked for the serial number of the bike, which Bob gave to him. Suddenly, the man on the other end of the line sounded different—maybe a little excited.

He said, "Can I get your name, address, and phone number? I'll call you right back."

Bob gave him the information but then felt kind of jittery after he had hung up the phone. *What was that all about?* he wondered. *Maybe some Hell's Angel owned the bike, and it was involved in some kind of crime. Or maybe it was stolen!*

A couple of hours went by, and Bob got a call. The man on the other end of the line identified himself as an executive with Harley Davidson Motorcycles and had a strange request.

"I'd like you to do something for me, Bob. Don't hang up, but I'd like you to go over to the bike, take the seat off, and turn it over. Tell me if anything is written there."

Bob complied with the instructions, picked up the phone again, and said, "Yeah, the words *The King* are written on the seat."

There was a brief pause on the line, and then the man from Harley Davidson said, "Bob, I am prepared to offer you $300,000 cash for that motorcycle right now. Do we have a deal?"

"No," Bob answered, "we don't have a deal. I need to find out what's going on here."

An hour later he got a call from a Hollywood celebrity who

was a collector of old cars and motorcycles. The celebrity offered Bob $500,000 for the bike. Bob later found out that the Harley in his garage originally belonged to Elvis Presley, "the king of rock and roll." It had been lost for years, and now that it had been rediscovered, it was a thing of great value.

An urban legend? Possibly. But it makes a point: That which was in the back of a garage under a tarp, purchased for thirty-five dollars, and thought of as having no value had suddenly become very valuable because of who had owned and ridden on that old Harley.

At Christmastime we celebrate the birth of the King—the real King—the King of the Jews and the King of the universe, Christ the Messiah, and our Savior. But like that old Harley, His birth wasn't much noted or valued at the time. For the most part, people missed that first Christmas.

They still do.

I remember reading an article in the newspaper about a man who had a Nativity scene set up on his front yard. You know the typical scene: Mary and Joseph, the little baby Jesus, and a few sheep thrown in. All of these figures had little lights in them.

Then one night some vandals came along and stole his little plastic baby Jesus with a ten-watt bulb inside. This guy got really stressed out about it. The local newspaper interviewed him, and in the article he pleaded with the robber to please bring Jesus back to him.

I read that and thought, *You know what buddy? Maybe you need to get a life. We're talking about a plastic replica here.*

But to him that was really important. In a broad sense, you might say this man was looking for Jesus. Unfortunately, his Jesus was a plastic baby with a light bulb inside. But at least he thought enough of Jesus to miss the plastic replica! Many other people at this time of year are working feverishly to remove any remembrance of Jesus from public view.

These are generally the same people who have tried to remove the "one nation under God" phrase from our pledge of allegiance, labored tirelessly to keep prayer out of our schools, gone to court to keep anyone from seeing the Ten Commandments posted in public view, and generally done everything they could to remove the name of Jesus Christ—or even the word *Christmas*—from their no-name holiday celebrations.

In Portland, Maine, a site manager for that city's housing authority recently attempted to clarify a new policy banning all religious celebrations or decorations. It mandated, "There shall be no angels, crosses, stars of David, or any other icons of religion displayed on the walls, floors, ceilings, *et cetera* upon your apartment buildings except within your own apartment." The dictum went on to decree that anything hanging on the inside of a resident's door was permissible, but nothing whatsoever was allowed on the outside, exposed to the hallway, because "it might offend someone."

Or how about the grade school principal in Sacramento, California, who strictly warned his teachers against attaching the word *Christmas* to any written materials within their classrooms?

In case you haven't noticed, the politically correct greeting at this time of the year is no longer "Merry Christmas" but the more generic, insipid "Happy Holidays."

I refuse to say Happy Holidays.

My recommendation? Say Merry Christmas to people—cheerfully, distinctly, politely, and without shame!

Or when you receive one of those wimpy "Happy Holidays" greetings, smile your brightest smile and say, "Why, thank you! And God bless you," or "Jesus loves you." We who belong to Jesus ought to have no shame in declaring His name or His love. We *own* Him in public, just as He owns us.

The attempt to remove every vestige of Christmas, however, has gone to almost unbelievable lengths. Now even the humble *snowflake* has been deemed offensive. In Saratoga Springs, New York, third graders at Division Street Elementary School saw their Christmas project confiscated by an indignant principal. Entering their classroom, he was struck with horror when he saw the boys and girls adorning an oversized Christmas ornament with colored photos of snowflakes. He quickly removed the offending item from sight, and there is no word as to whether the teacher was allowed to keep her job. (She probably had to attend sensitivity training.)

Others have banned poinsettias for alleged "religious connotations."

All of this seems incredibly sad to me.

But when you think about it, there's something even more sad than that. There are sincere believers in the Lord Jesus Christ who will lose sight of Him this year, during the very season set apart to honor His entry into our world.

MISSING PERSON

Did you ever feel as though you somehow lost God from your life? One day as you were going about your affairs, you suddenly realized that something seemed to be missing. And that's when it dawned on you that you hadn't given a single thought to God all day . . . or maybe for several days. That connection with Heaven you had always enjoyed seemed distant at best. It was almost as though He were gone.

I heard the story of a little boy who wandered into a local church. Wide-eyed, he saw all the candles lit for a time of prayer.

Misunderstanding the meaning of those symbols, he proceeded to blow out all of the candles and sing "Happy Birthday" to Jesus.

The minister who observed all this was incensed. When the boy walked out the doors, he followed him home. After the little guy went into his house, the minister knocked on the door, and the boy's mother answered.

"Yes, Reverend, what can I do for you?"

He replied, "Ma'am, I want to speak with your son. He has no respect for God whatsoever."

With a sigh, she said, "Okay, come on in. I'll get him."

The little boy walked slowly down the stairs from his room, coming to stand in front of the stern-faced man of the cloth.

"I have a question for you, son," he said. "Where is God?"

The boy didn't know what to say.

Again the minister leaned forward and said, "Little boy, I asked you a question. *Where is God?*"

At this, the boy's eyes went wide as saucers, and he started to tremble.

When the minister asked him one more time, the little boy bolted out of the room, ran upstairs, and slammed the door of his bedroom behind him.

His mother ran to his room and said, "Honey, what's wrong?"

"Mommy," her son said in a frightened voice, "they have lost God at that church, and they think I took Him!"

We can lose God in the holiday season. But here is something to consider: If you feel far from God, *guess who moved?* God hasn't gone anywhere . . . but maybe we have. And in the busyness of the season and in the so-called celebration of the birth of Christ, we can forget all about Him.

You know how it is. On Wednesday there's a white elephant gift exchange at the office. Then on Thursday there's that special Christmas movie you wanted to see with the family. And the weekend? Yikes! You haven't sent Christmas cards yet. And there's so much shopping to do! How will you ever get it all done?

And somewhere in it all, we lose track of our Lord.

Maybe there was a point in your life when you walked closely with the Lord, but in recent days, it seems like you've lost sight of Him.

A LOST LOVE

I'm reminded of the words of Jesus to the church of Ephesus in Revelation 2, where He says,

> I know your deeds, your hard work and your persever-
> ance. I know that you cannot tolerate wicked people, that

you have tested those who claim to be apostles but are not, and have found them false. You have persevered and have endured hardships for my name, and have not grown weary.

Yet I hold this against you: You have forsaken the love you had at first. Consider how far you have fallen! Repent and do the things you did at first. If you do not repent, I will come to you and remove your lampstand from its place. (verses 2–5, NIV)

To read this account, it sounds as though the First Church of Ephesus was a busy, active, productive church. They wouldn't tolerate false teaching and seemed to have all their doctrinal ducks in a row.

But somehow in all that activity, work, and study, they had lost sight of Jesus. And the Lord Himself had to say to them, "You have left your first love."

Work had taken the place of worship. Perspiration had taken the place of inspiration. So the Great Physician, our Lord Himself, wrote them a prescription for renewal or revival: "Consider how far you have fallen! Repent and do the things you did at first."

I sum it up like this. There are three Rs for getting right with God: remember, repent, repeat.

"GET BACK"

Maybe there was a time when you were closer to God, but now, for whatever reason, you're not in that place. You can remember what it was like. You read one of your old journals, and it seems to just overflow with love for Jesus. But now there's a distance.

What do you do? In the immortal words of Paul, John, George, and Ringo, "Get back, get back. Get back to where you once belonged." In other words, remember where you were and go back to that place.

Do you remember the way it was when you first came to Jesus Christ? Do you remember the passion, the excitement?

I saw a movie recently that included the testimonies of a group of young surfers who had all come to Christ. It was so refreshing to hear the stories of these young men who had come out of a life of partying, drugs, and all that other stuff that kids get themselves into.

Then one of them came to Christ and started telling all his friends about the Lord. And one by one, this whole group of friends gave their lives to Christ. Now they're all serving Him.

Some of these guys were very successful in their sport and had lots of honors and accolades thrown their way. They were making money and acquiring some fame. But at the same time, all of them admitted to an emptiness in their lives—an emptiness now filled to overflowing by a relationship with God through Jesus. And they were talking about how thrilling it was to have a Bible study and what a joy it was to pray together.

It reminded me of the thousands who have come to Christ through the years of our ministry in places all over the world. There's almost always evidence that something is different, that something has changed. There are changed priorities as you seek to know Him better and walk with Him more closely. You look forward to being with other believers at church and at Bible studies and at worship times. You're excited about getting alone with God in prayer.

Frankly, if these things don't draw you and excite you, that would tell me there's something spiritually wrong. It would tell me that maybe you need to get back to where you were—where you should be. *Remember* from where you have fallen. *Repent* and change your direction. And *repeat*, doing those things that you used to do when Jesus was number one in your life.

It's amazing how we can go through a day and never think about Jesus. In many ways we can live like practical atheists, with no thought of God whatsoever except when we get our food. "Oh yeah. Let's pray. Lord, uh, bless this food." *Hello. Good-bye.*

Have you lost sight of Jesus? As we enter a new year, let's make a real effort to remember Him by taking time for the Word of God. And by that I mean carve out time for Bible study. Don't just try to work it into your busy schedule. *Change* your busy schedule and make time for God's Word.

Let's remember Him by taking time each and every day for prayer—time to spend in the presence of God, listening to His voice as well as baring our hearts to Him and bringing our petitions to Him. The Bible says, "Men always ought to pray and not lose heart" (Luke 18:1).

Let's remember Him in our involvement in church with His people, not just working it in when we can find the time but understanding there is a priority in gathering with God's people for worship and prayer. Church is not just a place where we take in. It is also a place where we give out. It is a place to use the gifts that God has given to us, seek spiritual accountability, and listen to the advice that others can give us. It is also a place to invest our finances and share in what God is doing.

Remember Him also as you look for opportunities to share your faith with others. The Christmas season is such a natural time to speak about Jesus and to tell others about this One who has been born and was crucified and has risen from the dead.

Don't miss the *real* Christmas this Christmas.

Looking back into the biblical account, we can identify people or groups of people who certainly did miss the incredible significance of what was happening right in front of them.

PEOPLE WHO MISSED IT

The innkeeper

First there was a certain innkeeper. . . .

What the tired couple needed when they came into Bethlehem was a nice motel—or just any motel! As they walked through town, however, all they could see were "no vacancy" signs. They came to the inn where they had hoped to stay, but there was no room for them, and they were turned away.

Presumably it was an innkeeper who delivered this bad news. Clearly he could see that Mary was well along in her pregnancy and that she needed a clean and warm room in case she were to give birth. But he stood at the door of the inn and shook his head.

"Sorry," he said. "No room. Nothing available."

Frankly, it's hard for me to imagine a man being that heartless. Call me old-fashioned if you'd like, but I'm one of those people who believe that when a woman is headed toward a door, a man should open that door for her. I know very well that some women don't appreciate it these days, but I think there are still a lot of women who do. And if I'm seated in a train or a bus and a woman walks in with no place to sit, I give her my seat. It's a matter of common courtesy, especially if she is an older woman and certainly if she is a pregnant woman. I think we should go out of our way to assist a pregnant woman because of the discomfort that pregnancy brings. You want to make it a little easier for her.

So I have a difficult time with this innkeeper who turned away an obviously pregnant young woman and her husband. It seems like just simple human kindness would say, *Clear a space for these two. Put a roof over them. She could give birth tonight.*

In this woman's womb was the Creator of the universe in human form. And this guy was too busy to give them the time of day, much less a place of rest and shelter.

And if you were Joseph with the responsibility for this woman and the unborn child, you would find yourself saying, "Now what?"

As it turned out, there was a ramshackle little building—or perhaps a cave—behind the inn that was used as a stable for the animals. With no other options, it was there that Joseph finally sought shelter for the night.

It's easy to vilify a man like this innkeeper and think of him as a wicked man. That could have been the case. But more plausibly, I think he probably was just a very preoccupied and busy man. Occupied with making money, he had all the business he could handle that night and didn't take time to consider the right thing to do.

It reminds me of our country today and those who have no time to seek God. We invite people to church, and they reply, "Well, we're just too busy right now. We have so much to do."

We say, "Why don't you come to church with us on Christmas?"

And we hear replies like, "That's a nice idea but . . . we're going to a play" or "This movie just opened" or "We have to do a bit more shopping" or "We have another commitment."

I'm reminded of the psalmist who talked about those who couldn't be bothered with seeking the Lord. He wrote, "In all his thoughts there is no room for God" (Psalm 10:4, NIV).

So it is with many in today's world. Even on the day set aside to celebrate the birth of Jesus Christ, there's no time for Him at all. There's nothing left in the schedule. There's no time for faith. There's no room in the inn.

So the Savior of the world was born in a barn. But it wasn't Jesus who missed out, it was the innkeeper. Why did he miss out? Because he was interested in the bottom line: the dollar, the buck (or in his case, the shekel). So in the busyness of all that was going on with the census being taken, he missed Christmas. And he missed Christ, just like so many people today with all of the shopping and all of the parties and all of the events. They miss it.

The religious leaders

The religious teachers completely missed Jesus. Herod called these theological experts in after the wise men asked, "Where is He who has been born King of the Jews?"

They knew the answer all right. It was Bethlehem. They could quote chapter and verse to the evil king. And yet these men—the supposed guardians of spiritual truth in Israel—wouldn't bother to walk a few miles south to Bethlehem to find out if the Messiah of Israel had indeed been born.

At least Herod feared Jesus' authority—and he tried to nip it in the bud. The innkeeper could claim busyness and ignorance. But what about these men? They knew better. They knew the Word of God, and yet they did nothing to respond to it. They were indifferent. They were too busy with themselves to be concerned about Jesus. In fact, when His public ministry began, they became His principal adversaries.

For all practical purposes, these were the very men who were responsible for the execution of Jesus Christ. Why? Because He was a threat to their little religious empire. The Bible says they sent Him up to Pilate out of envy. They envied His authority. They envied the fact that people loved Him and hung on His every word. They envied the fact that He seemed to have a relationship with God that they lacked.

Addressing this at a later date, Jesus said, "Isaiah was right when he prophesied about you hypocrites; as it is written: 'These people honor me with their lips, but their hearts are far from me. They worship me in vain; their teachings are merely human rules'" (Mark 7:6-7, NIV).

They were looking for a different kind of messiah. They didn't want a messiah who would suffer and die on a cross for them. They were looking for someone who would support their religious system and their chosen way of living, someone who would cater to their whims and conform to their wishes, someone who would keep them in power.

There are many people like this today. They want Jesus, but they want Him on their terms.

They want the kind of Jesus they can control, the kind of Jesus who will never challenge them, the kind of Jesus who won't ask them to change their ways.

They want Heaven, but they don't want to talk about hell.

They want forgiveness, but they are unwilling to repent.

They want the cross, but they don't want Christ.

I heard a true story about a woman who went into a jewelry store and began looking at various crucifixes. After examining them for a while, she said to the jeweler, "Do you have any crosses without this little man on them?"

That's how it is for many people today. They want religion—but only according to their own sensibilities. They want truth—but only if it aligns with "their truth."

The fact is that religion can be a deadly trap. When all is said and done, more people will be sent to hell by religion than by all of the wicked and sinful vices this world has to offer.

King Herod

King Herod missed Christmas. In fact, he tried to stop it from happening. When the wise men said they were looking for the one who had been born King of the Jews, they couldn't have said a more provocative thing to this paranoid king and puppet of Rome. So he tried to kill Christ. He failed in that effort, of course, but he succeeded in killing untold numbers of baby boys in the process, bringing great sorrow and mourning to Bethlehem. Soon he, too, would be dead—and would face his Creator with blood-stained hands.

The Roman Empire

And then there was the entire empire of Rome. They had established the worldwide census, and Roman soldiers and officials were everywhere, making sure that everyone complied. They had a government and a bureaucracy capable of tracking the taxes of millions of citizens across the known world. But somehow they missed it when God Himself entered the Roman world and came to visit humanity. Busy with their other gods and the business of ruling an empire, they overlooked the One who would be greater than a thousand empires.

It's a warning to all of us.

It's possible to get a great many things right in life—the right college, the right career, the right city, the right neighborhood—and miss the most important thing of all.

7

DON'T LOSE JESUS

People get so psycho about getting good deals on certain electronic gift items.

As you may remember, an employee of Walmart in Long Island, New York, was trampled to death as the crowd waiting outside the door stampeded into the store to find a little savings. Other workers were also trampled as they tried to rescue the stricken man. At least four people, including a woman who was eight months pregnant, were taken to hospitals.

In Tennessee, yet another person was trampled at the entrance of a Toys R Us store when its doors were opened. Thankfully, this person survived. At another crowded Toys R Us in Palm Desert, California, two men pulled guns and shot each other to death after the women who were with them began to brawl.

Maybe we all should take a deep breath for a moment and remember what this time is all about.

I've never enjoyed the shopping aspect of Christmas. Not long ago I heard the story of a couple of men who decided to go sailing instead of Christmas shopping with their wives. So they got out their sailboat, launched it, and were making their way out into the ocean. As it happened, a big December storm slammed into them when they were out to sea, and despite their best efforts, the boat took on a lot of water. As they got close to shore, they were beached on a sandbar. Chest-deep in the freezing water, they tried mightily to free their boat from the sand, but the big waves kept slamming them against the side of the hull.

After their third or fourth attempt, one man was heard saying to the other, "Sure beats Christmas shopping, doesn't it?"

It seems as though we have certainly lost the name of Jesus somewhere in the confusion and chaos of the Christmas celebration. In much of our country, we have lost sight of an authentic Christmas altogether. In the process, I think we have also lost sight of God.

YOU HAVE HIS FULL ATTENTION

Whenever I am out and about with my granddaughter Stella, I have to keep my eye on her every moment—especially in a toy store. If you are with a child in a toy store and are not holding her hand, she will disappear in the blink of an eye. You will look up at something for what seems like a millisecond, look back, and the child will be gone. She will be darting up and down different aisles, checking everything out. As a result, I always keep my eye on Stella, even though she doesn't necessarily have her eye on me.

In the same way, we sometimes lose sight of God. It's not because He is rushing around or darting in and out of the galaxies; it's because *we* get distracted or absorbed in so many things. Then, when we finally look up again, it's hard to see Him.

But here's the good news: even though we lose sight of God, He never loses sight of us. Remember the blessing that the priests in the Old Testament were given to pray over the people? It went like this: "The Lord bless you and keep you; the Lord make His face shine upon you, and be gracious to you; the Lord lift up His countenance upon you, and give you peace" (Numbers 6:24–26).

It's an incredibly beautiful blessing and maybe even one that we have read or spoken over others. But have we really understood what it *means*? That phrase "*the Lord lift up His countenance*" could be translated "to look, to see, to know, to be interested in, to have one's full attention." Here, then, is what God is saying: "I will bless you, I will keep you, and you will have My full attention throughout the days of your life."

Have you ever been speaking to someone—maybe pouring out your heart to them—and they look distracted? Maybe as soon as you pause for breath, he pulls out his smartphone and starts checking his e-mails. Or, he actually will take a call while you're in the middle of unburdening your soul. He will say, "Could you hold that thought just for a second? . . . Hello? Hey! What's up? . . . No, I'm not doing anything. . . . Yeah. I'll get right back to you."

What you realize in that moment is that your "friend" really isn't all that interested in your life. He pretends to care for a moment or two, but he really doesn't. He's just looking for a reason to end the conversation and walk away.

Aren't you glad the Lord doesn't take phone calls when you're talking to Him? *Hello, Gabriel? Listen, I'll get right back to you. I'm in a conversation that I'll wrap up in a second or two. . . .*

When you are pouring out your heart to Him, He is taking in every word. Beyond that, He is weighing the emotions and thoughts you have behind the words. And He knows the thoughts and feelings you can't even express. His eyes aren't glancing around the room, and He isn't checking His watch. He is engaged with you 100 percent.

When that thought occurred to King David, it staggered him. He wrote these words in one of his psalms: "How precious it is, Lord, to realize that you are thinking about me constantly! I can't even count how many times a day your thoughts turn toward me. And when I waken in the morning, you are still thinking of me!" (Psalm 139:17–18, TLB).

In times of stress or disappointment, you might find yourself wondering whether God is even aware of what might be unfolding in your life. Count on it: He *is* aware. He knows your story and the million stories behind your story.

The essential message of Christmas is that God came to us. He took the initiative. He always is watching you, always caring for you.

You may remember the story from the gospel of Mark where Jesus dispatched His disciples across the Sea of Galilee while He stayed behind to pray:

> Later that night, the boat was in the middle of the lake, and he was alone on land. He saw the disciples straining at the oars, because the wind was against them. Shortly before dawn he went out to them, walking on the lake. (Mark 6:47–48, NIV)

They couldn't see Him, but He could see them, and He knew their situation. He knew the wind was against them. He knew they had exhausted themselves straining at the oars. He knew they were frightened and discouraged. Ultimately, He came to them across the stormy waters.

It's no different with you. He is watching you. He is praying for you. He knows when you feel outmatched, outgunned, and overwhelmed. And He will come to you, straight through your storm, even though you may have lost sight of Him in the night and in the swirling clouds.

There was a time in the life of Jesus when Mary and Joseph lost sight of Him for a few days.

WHERE IS JESUS?

It really happened: Mary and Joseph literally lost Jesus! They misplaced Him! They missed Him in the shuffle!

Jesus was twelve years old at the time, and Mary and Joseph had taken Him with them to the temple in Jerusalem for Passover. But somehow, in the busyness of the holiday celebration, they lost track of their boy. When they got down the road a good distance, they finally realized (to their alarm) that He wasn't with them.

In some ways, it presents a good parallel to the difficulty we have in keeping Jesus in focus at this time of year that is supposed to be about Him. With all the pressures and activities, in all the parties and celebrations and events, we might very well lose sight of the Lord.

A friend of mine told me about an incident with his little boy. One night when he and his son knelt for prayer by the little boy's bedside, the young lad prayed, "And God, thank You for sending Your only forgotten Son."

It was a mistake. He meant to say, "Your only *begotten* Son." It makes for a cute story, but there's some truth in what the little boy prayed. For many believers, even at Christmas, Jesus Christ has become God's only forgotten Son.

Let me illustrate. Let's say that it was your fortieth birthday and a large party was being given to celebrate that milestone. All of your friends come to the party, and there are presents in abundance and a huge cake with fancy writing in the frosting. Your friends get so into the occasion that they actually go out and record songs about you that repeat your name over and over.

So there it is: a big party and lots of excitement and hoopla. But somehow in all this commotion, no one remembered to invite you, the guest of honor, to your own party!

You assume that it was just an oversight, and you decide to show up at the party anyway, assured that once you arrive, all the guests will welcome you with open arms. You arrive at the house where you see your name emblazoned in lights, and you can hear your name being sung in song after song. But nobody responds to your knock at the door, and the door is locked. The music is so loud that they can't hear you, and the people are so busy that they don't see you. Finally you shrug your shoulders, walk away from your own party, and drive home.

This is a picture of Christmas for many of us today. We string our lights, decorate our trees, and run around buying gifts for those we love (and more gifts for those we don't love) because we feel pressured to do so. We go to countless events and run around like crazy people. But then we have to ask ourselves, *Has God's only begotten Son become God's only forgotten Son? Have I lost God at Christmas? Is that possible?*

Yes, it certainly is, and many of us have experienced such a loss, just as Joseph and Mary lost the boy Jesus in the milling crowds at Passover.

We don't know a lot about the upbringing of Jesus. We know He would have been raised by Joseph, His stepfather or guardian, though Joseph wasn't His biological father. He would have been taught the craft of carpentry because Joseph was a carpenter. As a result, Jesus would have been good with His hands.

He certainly would have been a hard worker and would have known how to build a table, a chair, a plow, or even a house. I am sure He was a master craftsman. Can you imagine Jesus, the One who created the world, doing shoddy work? I can't. He was what you might describe today as a blue-collar worker. He was a man who would go to the synagogue or temple on the Sabbath. He was obedient to His parents.

At the same time, however, there has never been a man who

walked the earth like Jesus, because He was God in human form. He never sinned, never lost His temper, and never did anything wrong at all. While He grew physically in the normal way, He never bounced back and forth between sin and obedience the way that you and I do. No, Jesus went from faith to faith, from grace to grace, from strength to strength, and from obedience to new levels of obedience. But at the same time, Dr. Luke pointed out that Jesus Christ the boy, and later the man, grew up physically, mentally, and spiritually.

This brings up an interesting question. Because Jesus was God, did He have the full knowledge of God when He was that little baby in the manger in Bethlehem? In other words, did He lie there in that little manger of straw and think, *I am the Creator of the universe*? Did He sit up in the manger and say words like these? "Hello, Mary, Joseph. How are you? Good to see you. Listen, I need a little help getting out of this manger. By the way, could someone change my diaper? I would really appreciate that."

No! He was God, but He also was an authentic human baby. The almighty Creator of all things, with unlimited strength, had chosen to be dependent on a mother for His nourishment and nurture as any other little baby would.

We know that He grew in height, in strength, and in wisdom over a period of time. Luke 2:40 says that "the child grew up healthy and strong. He was filled with wisdom, and God's favor was on him" (NLT).

Then in Luke 2:52 we read that "as Jesus continued to grow in body and mind, he grew also in the love of God and of those who knew him" (PH).

Joseph, Mary, and Jesus had traveled to Jerusalem for the annual Passover celebration. After spending several days among the thousands of Jews thronging the capital, they packed up and headed for home. Back in those days, the men would travel after the women. The women would go on ahead, and the men would follow along behind. So Joseph no doubt assumed that young Jesus was traveling with Mary, and Mary assumed that He was with Joseph.

When they had gone a day's journey down the road, however, they discovered to their shock and dismay that Jesus was absent. He hadn't been with the women, and He hadn't been with the men. He hadn't been with the cousins or the neighbors. No one had seen Him.

They had forgotten Jesus! Can you imagine that conversation?

"So where is Jesus?"

"He's with you—isn't He?"

"I don't have Jesus. I thought He was with you."

"I don't have Him, either."

"Where is Jesus? How can we lose Jesus?"

"Where did you see Him last?"

"I saw Him at the temple."

"Well, let's go back there."

This brings up the point that Jesus was ordinary in appearance. He didn't glow in the dark or have a shining halo over His head. If that had been true, He would have been easy to find. Mary and Joseph could have simply said, "Anybody see a glowing child? He's the one with the halo and the shiny robe. You can't miss Him."

But no, Jesus didn't glow. It would appear from the Scriptures that He was as ordinary a man as you could imagine. In fact, when Judas Iscariot went to the Garden of Gethsemane to identify Him to the authorities, he had to basically say, "He'll be the one I kiss. That's the one you need to arrest."

Jesus didn't stand out from the crowd. In Isaiah 53 we read, "But in our eyes there was no attractiveness at all, nothing to make us want him" (verse 2, TLB).

So in all the hubbub of a huge religious celebration, Mary and Joseph had forgotten the One whom the Passover was all about. They went back and eventually found Him in the temple, "sitting in the midst of the teachers, both listening to them and asking them questions" (Luke 2:46). When Joseph and Mary tried to correct Him, He said, "Did you not know that I must be about My Father's business?" (verse 49).

To me, this story pictures today's Christmas celebrations. We get caught up in all the noise and activities and confusion, and we forget the One whom we claim to be honoring. He gets left behind somewhere in the crowd.

Don't lose God this Christmas. Don't forget about Jesus in all the parties and celebrations—and even in the church services. Find those quiet moments in quiet places where you can draw near to Him, speak to Him, and hear His voice.

LOSING HIM IN OUR BUSYNESS

Sometimes when we get busy, we start to cut out what we consider to be nonessentials. People will say, "I'm really swamped right now. I don't have time to do everything that I normally do. I don't have time to read the Bible. I don't have time to pray."

It always interests me when I hear people say things like that. Really? You don't have time to read your Bible? Maybe you should *make* time for that. Maybe there are some things you could cut out so you would have a little bit more time for Bible study. You always will find time for what is important to you, no matter what. And the last thing you ought to cut out is your time of Bible study and your time of prayer as you're getting ready for the day. But often that is the first thing to get tossed out of the daily schedule.

Sometimes we can even get too busy doing right or "spiritual" things. The classic example of this is the story of Mary and Martha when Jesus came to visit. Jesus liked spending time with the two sisters and their brother, Lazarus. And Martha probably was an excellent cook. Jesus liked to go over to her home. I wonder if He ever just showed up and said, "Hey, Mary and Martha, how's it going? I brought the twelve disciples with me. Could you make us lunch?"

Maybe Martha would say, "Lord, it would be my privilege. You guys sit down. Make yourselves comfortable." And they all would wait while she whipped up one of her famous feasts. That was Martha. She showed her love for Jesus in a tangible, practical way.

Mary, who also loved Jesus with all her heart, was a little different from her sister and may have been a little more tuned in spiritually. On one occasion when Jesus showed up, Martha made a beeline for the kitchen and started throwing pots and pans around, planning to prepare a feast fit for a king . . . because, well, He *is* a King.

In John's gospel account, we read that Mary didn't head for the kitchen with her sister but instead planted herself at Jesus' feet, not wanting to miss a single word. Martha, red-faced and perspiring as she chopped up meat and vegetables and started baking bread, glanced into the living room from time to time to see her sister paying rapt attention to the Lord and forgetting all else.

It made Martha mad. Finally unable to contain her frustration any longer, she burst into the room and interrupted the Lord's words. Can you imagine? There was God Almighty sharing truths of eternity in the living room, and she interrupted to say, in effect, "Excuse me, excuse me. Sorry to bother You, but I could use a little help in the kitchen. Lord, would You tell my sister to get up and start helping me a little?"

I love how Jesus answered His friend: "Martha, dear Martha, you're fussing far too much and getting yourself worked up over nothing. One thing only is essential, and Mary has chosen it—it's the main course, and won't be taken from her" (Luke 10:41–42, MSG).

The fact is that we can become so busy working *for* God that we miss time *with* God. When we think about people who are far from God, we tend to think of those who left the fellowship of believers, stopped reading their Bibles, and then made a series of really stupid and destructive life decisions. But don't fool yourself. You can be attending church every Sunday, serving on three church committees, and still lose sight of Jesus.

It reminds me of the story of the prodigal sons. (There actually were *two* prodigals in the story Jesus told.) One went out to a far country, wasted all of his money on crazy living, came to his senses, returned home, and was welcomed by his father. The other prodigal son never left home at all. But he was resentful to the core when his brother came back and was given a full pardon, and he let his dad know it. In reality, even though he showed up at the breakfast table every day and punched in on time at work, his heart was miles and miles from the heart of his father.

A prodigal, then, can be outside the church or inside the church.

In the account in Luke 2, Mary and Joseph lost Jesus and started looking for Him. Where did they finally find Him? Right where they last left Him! He was still there.

It's the same with us. Maybe, if you were honest, you'd have to say there was a time in your life when you were spiritually stronger and more excited about your faith in Christ than you are today.

You might say (with regret), "Well, yes, there was a time when I was a younger person and my fervor for God and passion for Christ were much greater than they are now. But that was a different time and season. I'll probably never be able to recover that again."

Really? I beg to differ. I think you can recover that lost passion. Why not do what Mary and Joseph did? Go back to the last place you were with Him. Go back to that place where you lost Him. He's still there! He is in the same place He always has been, and He is there right now, waiting for you to return. God hasn't gone anywhere. You are the one who moved off in a different direction and lost sight of Him.

There are some things you never outgrow, never get beyond. Being a Christian isn't rocket science; it's really not that complicated. God has told us there are certain disciplines we must have in our lives if we want to grow spiritually. And one of those is regular Bible study. You don't get past that.

Yet I am amazed at how there are believers who have known the Lord for years and can't remember the last time they cracked open the Bible and asked God to speak to them. And then they say, "God never talks to me!" Maybe it's because they so rarely open up His Book! God *will* speak to our hearts if we open His Word and diligently seek Him.

I know people who have no prayer life to speak of. You don't get beyond that! No believer can honestly say, "Well, I used to pray, but I don't need to anymore."

Yes, you do. Listen to Paul's commands to the Thessalonians: "Rejoice always, pray without ceasing, in everything give thanks; for this is the will of God in Christ Jesus for you" (1 Thessalonians 5:16–18).

You say, "How does that work? I'd never get anything done if I spent all day and all night on my knees."

That is not what Paul is talking about. What he is saying is to live your life in an attitude of prayer. Keep the contact open. Shoot up prayers to Him on the details of your day and be listening for His voice as He speaks to your heart.

Were you ever talking to someone on the phone, and he or she neglected to end the call? You can hear that person talking and walking around, but he or she has no idea the line is still open. This verse is saying to do this deliberately with God. Don't hang up on Him. Keep that call going all day and all night. (And by the way, you'll never run out of minutes. God always will pick up the bill for that.)

And then there are those Christians who aren't even in fellowship with God's people at all. Where did Mary and Joseph find Jesus? They found Him in the house of God. Where are you going to find Jesus? In the same place! I'm not talking about a particular building. The house of God is wherever God's people are gathered together—for worship, for Bible study, for fellowship, for service, and all the rest. If you aren't plugged into a local fellowship where people know your face and your name, it will result in your spiritual downfall.

The Bible says, "And let us not neglect our meeting together, as some people do, but encourage and warn one another, especially now that the day of his return is drawing near" (Hebrews 10:25, NLT).

How clear is that? Christ could not only return in our lifetime, but He could return this year—or tomorrow. So when He comes, let Him find you with God's people, worshiping, growing, and encouraging one another.

Have you lost sight of Jesus in this season of your life? Have you overlooked Him in this hectic, sometimes pressured Christmas season? Maybe you have simply forgotten about Him as the years have passed by. I have good news for you: God has not forgotten about you!

You'll find Him right where you left Him.

He is there for you at this very moment.

Do you hear His voice?

He says, "Be still, and know that I am God."

8

WHAT THE WISE MEN UNDERSTOOD

We know the Christmas card image so well. There are always three of them, wearing turbans and riding on camels, silhouetted against a night sky. A huge, magnificent star blazes on the horizon. Tradition has given them names: Gaspar, Melchior, and Balthasar. They even have their own song to sing (in three-part harmony) as they plod along through the sandy wastes, seeking a newborn King:

> We three kings of Orient are
> Bearing gifts we traverse afar
> Field and fountain, moor and mountain
> Following yonder star.

The Bible, however, never says there were only three, doesn't mention camels, and doesn't give them names.

Let's peel this tradition back, and let's find out who these mysterious men from the East really were and what they have to teach us about worship.

The Bible calls them *Magi*. We get our English words *magic* and *magician* from this same term. These were men who consulted the stars and were experts in both astronomy and astrology. Rulers, kings, and pharaohs sought out their counsel and guidance. In contrast to the seers, prophets, and priests of the Scriptures, the Magi used sorcery, wizardry, and witchcraft, combining their science and mathematics with delvings into the occult. Over the years, their religious and political influence continued to grow until they became the most prominent and powerful group of advisers in the Medo-Persian and Babylonian empires.

These Magi, then, steeped in occultism and false religion, became very powerful, and were almost like royalty themselves. They wouldn't have worn the pajama-and-bathrobe kind of outfits (with the pointy shoes) that we see depicted on Christmas cards; they would have dressed in a way befitting their status and high office. And they wouldn't have ridden camels. They probably would have entered Jerusalem astride magnificent Arabian stallions. Most likely, they had a small army riding with them for protection. No wonder they created such a stir when that whole resplendent cavalcade rode through the gates of Jerusalem! It was like a foreign army coming in. Most likely, no one had ever seen anything like it.

To top it off, the question they immediately started asking must have swept through the streets like a stiff wind: "Where is He who has been born King of the Jews?" In no time at all, the question went viral!

And here is one more blow to our cherished images: The wise men were not present at the manger in Bethlehem on the night Jesus was born. Shepherds, yes. Wise men, no. The Bible says in Matthew 2:11, "And when they [the wise men] had come into *the house* [not the stable], they saw *the young Child* [not the Baby] with Mary His mother, and fell down and worshiped Him. And when they had opened their treasures, they presented gifts to Him: gold, frankincense, and myrrh" (emphasis added).

Nevertheless, these wise men from the East knew something that Herod and most others would never know: this little toddler in a tiny, humble house, born to common, working-class people, would one day rule the world.

The Magi brought Him gifts befitting a king: gold, frankincense, and myrrh. (Just a little note here about these gifts. You can safely bet they weren't wrapped in paper. Why do I say that? Because there were two important characteristics about those who gave the gifts: first, they were wise, and second, they were *men*. Men hate wrapping gifts.)

These Magi, pagan though they may have been, understood something right off the top that many people today never understand. They understood that Christmas is about worship.

The religious leaders in Jerusalem knew the Scriptures well enough to point the Magi in the right direction in their search for this newborn King:

When Herod the king heard this, he was troubled, and
all Jerusalem with him. And when he had gathered all
the chief priests and scribes of the people together, he
inquired of them where the Christ was to be born.

So they said to him, "In Bethlehem of Judea, for thus it
is written by the prophet:

'But you, Bethlehem, in the land of Judah,

Are not the least among the rulers of Judah;

For out of you shall come a Ruler

Who will shepherd My people Israel.' "

(Matthew 2:3–6)

Now they had a specific direction: Bethlehem, less than twenty
miles away. But how would they find the one particular Child among
all the children of that town and that region?

God sent the star ahead of them:

When they heard the king, they departed; and behold, the
star which they had seen in the East went before them, till
it came and stood over where the young Child was. When
they saw the star, they rejoiced with exceedingly great joy.
(verses 9–10)

When they received that specific direction from God, they were overcome with joy. Picture your most joyful moment in life and then multiply it by ten. These men had traveled vast distances through desolate and dangerous lands over many weeks, and now they were receiving strong confirmation that they were right on track and right on schedule. They would be granted the privilege of seeing a King whose destiny had been written in the stars.

What did they do when they finally found the house and the young Child? They fell down and worshiped Him.

Let me ask you a question: What would make this a perfect Christmas for you? Maybe you're thinking, *If I could just get this one thing I've really been hoping for—I left a detailed map for my parents so they could find the store. . . . I sent an e-mail with a link so that my wife could order it online. . . . I left a hint in my husband's briefcase.*

Or maybe it would be a perfect Christmas for you if your loved one really enjoys the gift you gave, the one you have been scheming about and planning for over the course of almost a year. If he or she is truly surprised or touched or excited or blown away—ah, that would just make the day for you.

The trouble is, the events of life hardly ever live up to our expectations. And Christmas is usually loaded up with all kinds of expectations. We hope the relationship with the in-laws will go better. We hope the dinner will come together the way we planned it. We hope everyone will get along. We hope that our hearts will be overflowing with emotions of nostalgia or peace or happiness.

Maybe these things will happen, and maybe they won't. But placing our hopes and desires on events turning out a certain way is usually a recipe for a big letdown.

The wise men, however, were particularly wise in the way they celebrated the birth of the King. They worshiped Him. But it wasn't just saying Merry Christmas to people on the street or humming "We Three Kings" when they got up in the morning. The Bible says they fell down and worshiped Him. In other words, they gave themselves completely over to praising and adoring the young King.

Another version of Matthew 2:11 says, "They entered the house and saw the child in the arms of Mary, his mother. Overcome, they kneeled and worshiped him" (MSG).

Immediately afterward, they opened their treasure bags and presented the Child with their precious gifts. Soon after this, God warned them in a dream not to go back through Jerusalem but to go home a different way. So they were still receiving direction from on high! God still was directing their path.

Do you think these men went home disappointed? Do you think they left Bethlehem feeling deflated or let down or depressed?

Far from it! I think this must have been the crowning event of their whole lives. Through all their years, they would talk about the star, the young King, and the opportunity they had been given to worship Him with all their hearts and offer Him gifts.

This is one activity that never will disappoint. Wholehearted worship of Jesus Christ, giving Him your best, giving Him yourself, always will fill your soul rather than deplete it.

The truth is, however, everyone worships at Christmas.

They may be politically correct and not even utter the word *Christmas*. They may not have a Nativity scene or even an inflated Santa Claus on their front lawn. It doesn't matter. Skeptics worship. Humbugs worship. Atheists and agnostics worship. Radical environmentalists, feminists, and mainstream media personalities worship. Conservative republicans and liberal democrats and confirmed independents worship. Even lawyers worship.

You say, "Greg, I beg to differ with you. Some of those people you mentioned don't worship at all."

But I didn't say they worship *God*. I said they worship. Everyone bows at the altar of something. They may not call it a deity, but it is something they are committed to and passionate about, something they believe in. Some people bow at the altar of material things. They worship their possessions: a car, a house, a boat, a bank account. Those are their gods.

Other people worship their own bodies. They've never met a mirror they didn't love. They spend hours studying exotic diets or sculpting their bodies at the gym or injecting strange things into their faces to remove wrinkles. Their own physical appearance is their god.

Other people worship a god of their own making. They say things like this: "Well, *my* god would never judge a person for doing something wrong. *My* god is all-loving and all-caring and all-tolerant."

But what god is that? In effect, they have created a god in their own image and according to their own notions of right and wrong.

But here is the problem: You can bow at these altars, but none of these gods are able to save you. None of these gods will help you. And quite frankly, none of these gods are worthy of your worship. There is only one God who is worthy of your worship: the living, triune God—Father, Son, and Holy Spirit.

How then, do we do it? How do we worship the Lord?

One way is by singing—perhaps some of the great carols of the season. That's one of the things I love about the Christian faith: we have all the killer songs! Why is that? Because we have something worth singing about. There is victory and joy and hope and celebration and honor in the songs we sing. What's more, all our singing here is just a warm-up act for eternity. Take a moment to contemplate the awesome scene described in Revelation 5:

> Then I looked, and I heard the voice of many angels around the throne, the living creatures, and the elders; and

the number of them was ten thousand times ten thousand, and thousands of thousands, saying with a loud voice:

> "Worthy is the Lamb who was slain
> To receive power and riches and wisdom,
> And strength and honor and glory and blessing!"

And every creature which is in heaven and on the earth and under the earth and such as are in the sea, and all that are in them, I heard saying:

> "Blessing and honor and glory and power
> Be to Him who sits on the throne,
> And to the Lamb, forever and ever!"

Then the four living creatures said, "Amen!" And the twenty-four elders fell down and worshiped Him who lives forever and ever. (verses 11–14)

The elders fell down and worshiped the Lord, just as the wise men did at the little house where Jesus was. And as you and I worship Him with all our hearts, we can enter into that joy that will never, never fade.

Human beings that we are, however, we don't always feel like praising the Lord. In fact, if the truth were known, it is sometimes the *last* thing we feel like doing. Yet that is the very time when our praise and thanksgiving mean the most. Hebrews 13:15 tells us, "Through Jesus, therefore, let us continually offer to God a sacrifice of praise—the fruit of lips that openly profess his name" (NIV).

When we praise God even when we don't feel like it, when we praise God through our disappointment or sorrow or tears, we are offering a sacrifice that pleases Him. Think what it means to you when someone you care about gives you a gift or card, looks you in the eyes, and says, "I love you." That expression, if you know it's really from the heart, means more than the gift, doesn't it? In the same way, the Lord likes to hear it when we say to Him, "Lord, I love you" and express that in our worship and our praise.

But that is not the only way that we can show our praise to God and offer our worship to the Lord. Another way that we worship God is through serving others, because one of the ways the word *worship* is translated in the Bible is "to serve and minister."

We looked at Hebrews 13:15, which speaks about the sacrifice of praise. But the very next verse goes on like this: "And do not forget to do good and to share with others, for with such sacrifices God is pleased" (verse 16, NIV).

A popular paraphrase of that same verse says this: "Make sure you don't take things for granted and go slack in working for the common good; share what you have with others. God takes particular pleasure in acts of worship—a different kind of 'sacrifice'—that take place in kitchen and workplace and on the streets" (MSG).

Most of us think of worship as what we do when we sing our songs and hymns, close our eyes, and lift our hands. And indeed, that can be worship. But worship also can be that meal you cook for a sick friend or that clothing or financial help you provide for someone in need.

I remember when I was in Billy and Ruth Graham's home in North Carolina years ago, before she went to Heaven. Ruth had placed a sign over her kitchen sink that read, "Divine service is conducted here three times a day." It's true. Even washing dishes for your family or friends can be an act of worship.

BRINGING OUR GIFTS TO HIM

Another way that we can worship is through our giving to the Lord. In Matthew 2:11 we read that the Magi, "when they had opened their treasures, they presented gifts to Him: gold, frankincense, and myrrh."

When you get a gift for someone, you start thinking about it ahead of time, don't you? If you really care about that person, you put some thought and care into it. You reflect on what you know about that individual and try to come up with something that would be a good fit and represent your love for him or her. You search for that gift. You set money aside and save for it. And then you go out and find it and bring it home.

When we think of the gift of Jesus' coming to Earth to die for our sins, it wasn't an afterthought with God or an impulse. The Bible says that Jesus was "slain from the foundation of the world" (Revelation 13:8). What does that mean? It means that long before there was a little town of Bethlehem or a garden called Eden or even a planet called Earth, a decision was made in the councils of eternity that God would come to Earth as a man to redeem His creation.

Why? Because God knew that man would blow it. God knew that Adam and Eve would eat the forbidden fruit. The Lord knew that we would sin and that if He was to have a relationship with His fallen creation, there would have to be an atonement. A sacrifice had to be made. It was all part of God's plan from the very beginning. That is how much thought He put into the gift He gave to each of us: the gift of eternal life.

I don't understand people who go to someone's birthday party without some kind of present in hand. It's always seemed to me that if I am invited to a party for someone, I am there to celebrate that person, and I ought to bring something. It doesn't have to be expensive or a big deal. It might just be a handmade card. It might be a cappuccino from Starbucks. I just don't want to walk through the door of my friend's house empty-handed on the day that he or she is being honored.

Everyone knows that Christmas is the Lord Jesus' birthday party. Should we enter the celebration empty-handed? What do we give to God? What does He really want?

Answer: He wants you.

That is the gift you can give to the Lord as you celebrate His birth. You can give yourself.

Paul said in Romans 12:1, "I urge you, brothers and sisters, in view of God's mercy, to offer your bodies as a living sacrifice, holy and pleasing to God—this is your true and proper worship" (NIV). Another version of that same verse says, "So here's what I want you to do, God helping you: Take your everyday, ordinary life—your sleeping, eating, going-to-work, and walking-around life—and place it before God as an offering. Embracing what God does for you is the best thing you can do for him" (MSG).

Bring your life to God.

Bring your time to God.

Bring your health to God.

Bring your family to God.

Bring your worries and concerns to God.

Bring your future to God.

Say, "Lord, this is what I offer to You."

Why do I do this? Because God is good, and He is worthy of my praise. The Bible says, "Oh, give thanks to the LORD, for He is good! For His mercy endures forever" (Psalm 107:1). That verse doesn't say, "Give thanks to the Lord because you've had a good year" or "Give thanks to the Lord because everything is going so well in your life."

The truth is that events in our lives don't always go well. As residents of a broken planet, we experience pain, disappointments, setbacks, and sorrows. But God is still good and worthy of our praise.

What are you worshiping? If you are bowing at the altar of Christmas this year, you will be deeply disappointed because Christmas the holiday cannot deliver on its promises. It can never, never live up to all the hype. It can't bring you inner peace, much less peace on earth. It can't bring you the joy and fulfillment you crave. Christmas the holiday always will let you down.

What is Christmas at its worst? It is a crass, commercial, empty, exhausting, and very expensive ritual that drags on endlessly for months. And then bills come due.

What is Christmas at its best? It is a promise of things to come—a glimpse of what still lies in our future. The beauty . . . the worshipful music . . . the adoring angels . . . the love . . . the warmth . . . the security . . . the nearness of God . . . the promise . . . the gathering of friends and family . . . It is all promised to us in a life to come. Yes, we get a glimpse of it now. But more is coming later.

What we need this year is not the promise of Christmas. That is a promise filled with holes and disappointment. What we need is the promise of Christ. We need the Messiah, not merriment. We need God, not goodwill. We need His presence, not just presents. We need the living, radiant, all-powerful, resurrected Jesus Christ, not a figurine in a manger scene.

Anything or anyone else will fall short of this.

If you worship a god of your own making, then he or she or it will disappoint you. But if you worship the true and living God, He never will disappoint you—not now and not in a trillion years.

Here is the thing that we often overlook when we think about the birth of Jesus: The beautiful Child born in the manger in Bethlehem was born to die. It is hard for us to think about the fact that those soft baby hands would one day grow into the hands of a strong man and have spikes driven through them. It's difficult for us to consider the fact that those little feet of the baby Jesus would one day be nailed to a cross of wood. It gives us pain to remember that the soft little forehead of the baby Jesus in the manger, so loved by His mother, would one day be crowned with thorns. This Child came with a purpose. From the moment He stepped foot on this planet, Jesus Christ lived in the shadow of the cross. He was born to die so that we might live.

RED

Those wise men had it right when they brought the unusual gifts of gold, frankincense, and myrrh. What kind of gifts are those to give to a kid? But they had an insight into why He came. They gave Him gold because that Child would one day reign as King. They gave Him frankincense because they recognized that He would become a High Priest, representing people to God. And they brought Him myrrh, which was the most bizarre gift of all. Myrrh was used for embalming! Why would you bring something so morbid, so inappropriate, to a young child? Because they recognized that this King, this High Priest, would die for our sins.

And He would give to us the ultimate gift: His very life.

9

THE MAN WHO TRIED TO STOP CHRISTMAS

Christmas, so we have assumed, is about love, peace, harmony, and the whole family gathered around a crackling fire, sipping warm cocoa.

That's the picture we've developed in our culture through the years, but that is not the true essence of Christmas. That isn't what the real Christmas story is all about.

Christmas is actually about conflict. It always has been, and it always will be.

In one of the latter chapters of this book, we will look at a startling passage in Revelation. It depicts a pregnant woman who is pursued by a powerful Dragon that seeks her death. As she prepares to give birth to the Child, the Dragon hovers over her, wanting to destroy the Baby.

That is Christmas from a heavenly perspective. The woman in that picture is the nation of Israel, the Child is the Lord Jesus Christ, and the Dragon is Satan. That gives you a big picture of what was really happening when God sent His Son into the world. The Devil opposed it and wanted to stop it, at all costs.

This dynamic is still in play today. In fact, it's growing more fierce (and desperate) as time goes by. You can see this same spirit—this hostility toward Christ and Christmas—sprouting up on all sides, and it escalates with each passing year. More Nativity scenes are being removed from public places every year. Atheists have been emboldened to put up billboards around the country, attacking the Christian faith. The city of Eugene, Oregon, banned Christmas trees in public spaces. This past year in Times Square, a giant, full-color ad asked the question "Who needs Christ during Christmas?" and included an answer: "nobody."

These are all symptoms of a trend that will grow more and more intense as we enter our planet's last days.

Mark this: Jesus did not come to bring a mind-numbing, self-indulgent peace on earth that is devoid of truth. Yes, we all remember what the angels declared to the shepherds keeping watch over their flocks on the night Christ was born: "Glory to God in the highest, and on earth peace, goodwill toward men!" (Luke 2:14).

But what does that mean? A better rendering of that passage would read, "On earth peace, goodwill toward men *among whom God is pleased.*" In other words, the only way we will have peace on earth is when men and women are pleasing to God.

Peace on Earth? Listen to what Jesus said in Luke 12:51–53:

Do you think I have come to bring peace to the earth? No, I have come to divide people against each other! From now on families will be split apart, three in favor of me, and two against—or two in favor and three against.

> "Father will be divided against son
>   and son against father;
> mother against daughter
>   and daughter against mother;
> and mother-in-law against daughter-in-law
>   and daughter-in-law against mother-in-law." (NLT)

This may not sound much like a Christmas message, but it is actually better than a Christmas message. It is New Testament Christianity—with its sharp division between light and darkness, good and evil, and righteousness and unrighteousness.

What we are seeing played out in our culture with these renewed attacks on the name of Jesus and even the celebration of Christmas is, in reality, a battle of the gods. It is the God of the Bible, the true and living God, against "the ruler of this world" (John 16:11).

So no, we shouldn't be surprised by the conflict we see around us. What might surprise us is that it's through conflict that we find peace.

Someone says, "What do you mean, Greg? Isn't that contradictory?"

No, not in the ultimate sense. Here is what I mean. If your family is like most families, it will be made up of both believers and nonbelievers. At times like Christmas, perhaps, you try to avoid subjects that might cause arguments or disagreements, but they inevitably come. Eventually, however, the topic of faith in Christ comes up, and some harsh words are spoken. Someone in your family might say something like, "We liked you better the old way. You were a lot more fun when we all drank together and did the things we used to do. Now you're acting pious and holier-than-thou. You've ruined Christmas for the rest of us."

Does this sort of discussion lead to peace? It can!

It's like when someone walks into a room and flips on a light switch, changing the whole dynamic in the room.

Some people will say, "Turn that off! We like it dark!"

There is such a contrast between light and the gloominess of a dark room that some people would rather pull back into the dim shadows. Sometimes you don't even have to *say* anything to make them uncomfortable. Your very presence as a Christian offends and irritates them.

How do you respond? Just hold your ground and keep praying for the nonbelievers in your family, and don't be upset or disheartened by a little conflict. Those individuals, as they consider your life and contrast it with their own, may be closer to Christ than you ever would guess. The very conflict may eventually lead them into peace with God.

THE BATTLE RAGES ON

This whole battle over Christmas in our culture has its roots all the way back to the beginning of history. After Satan caused the fall of Adam and Eve in the Garden, God spoke the very first messianic prophecy in the Bible. In Genesis 3:15 He told the Evil One, "From now on you and the woman will be enemies, as will your offspring and hers. You will strike his heel, but he will crush your head" (TLB).

Through the years, Satan watched for that Coming One with hatred and fear. He wanted to stop the Christ from being born because he knew the Messiah would be his doom.

Red is the color of Christmas—not because of red candles or a red-suited Santa or red ribbons around a package. Red is the color of Christmas because of the blood of Jesus Christ that would be poured out as the payment for our sins.

The red blood of Jesus tells the story of Satan's furious attempts to at first prevent the birth of Christ, and failing that, to maneuver for His death and destruction by the Roman overlords. Little did the

Devil realize that Christ's death and resurrection would be the very things that would seal his doom.

HEROD, SATAN'S UNWITTING ALLY

History might call him "Herod the Great," but a more accurate title might have been "Herod the Cruel" or maybe "Herod the Paranoid." This puppet king of Israel reigned in Jerusalem during the births of John the Baptist and Jesus. A portion of his story unfolds in Matthew 2.

Herod was raised in a well-connected family and was destined for a life of ruthless politics and power brokering. At age twenty-five, he was named the governor of Galilee, a very high position for such a young man. The Romans had high hopes that he would bring some calmness and control over the Jews in that troubling province they called Palestine.

In 40 BC, the Roman Senate gave Herod the title "king of the Jews," of which he was very proud. He became so attached to that image of himself that he couldn't bear any thought of a challenger to his throne, as we will soon see.

This was a man who was addicted to power and known for his cold and heartless cruelty. Anyone whom he perceived as even a distant threat to his rule would be quickly eliminated. History tells us that this blood-stained ruler murdered his brother-in-law, his mother-in-law, two of his own sons, and his favorite wife (he had many). He murdered out of spite to stay in power. Human life meant nothing to him.

There have always been such power-hungry, blood-thirsty rulers in our world. In fact, Herod reminds me of the present-day dictator of North Korea, Kim Jong Un. He recently had his uncle murdered in a barbaric way and has killed many of that nation's citizens for imagined or trivial offenses. There is great persecution of the church of Jesus Christ in that troubled nation. Kim Jong Un is something like a modern-day Herod—with a nuclear arsenal.

The historian Josephus called Herod "barbaric." Another dubbed him the "malevolent maniac." On one occasion he had the most distinguished citizens of Israel arrested, giving orders that upon his death they should be executed. Why would he do such a thing? It was to guarantee that it would be a day of great mourning in Israel when he died.

Herod also was known to be a great builder. He saw himself as a miniature Caesar, building seven palaces and seven theaters. One of those theaters seated 9,500 people. He constructed stadiums for sporting events, built the beautiful port city of Caesarea, and created the stronghold of Masada. Herod's crowning achievement as a builder was the second temple in Jerusalem. This was the temple that was standing when Jesus was engaged in His public ministry. It took forty-six years to build and was one of the wonders of the ancient world.

Imagine, then, the shock the disciples felt when Jesus gestured toward that monumental temple and said, "Do you see all these things? . . . Truly I tell you, not one stone here will be left on another; every one will be thrown down" (Matthew 24:2, NIV).

And within just a few years, in AD 70, that prophecy was literally fulfilled.

At the time of Christ's birth, Herod the Great, the so-called king of the Jews, wasn't feeling great at all. In fact, he was slowly dying from a terrible disease. Historians tell us that his body was wracked by convulsions, that his skin was covered with open sores, and that he was rapidly losing his mind. Nevertheless, he was still king! And in that day and time, being king counted for a great deal.

It was at this troubled time in Herod's life that word came to him of a party of foreign dignitaries who had come into town from the distant East. This is where Matthew picks up the story.

HEROD AND THE WISE MEN

Now after Jesus was born in Bethlehem of Judea in the days of Herod the king, behold, wise men from the East came to Jerusalem, saying, "Where is He who has been born King of the Jews? For we have seen His star in the East and have come to worship Him."

When Herod the king heard this, he was troubled, and all Jerusalem with him. And when he had gathered all the chief priests and scribes of the people together, he inquired of them where the Christ was to be born.

So they said to him, "In Bethlehem of Judea, for thus it is written by the prophet:

'But you, Bethlehem, in the land of Judah,
Are not the least among the rulers of Judah;
For out of you shall come a Ruler
Who will shepherd My people Israel.' "

Then Herod, when he had secretly called the wise men, determined from them what time the star appeared. And he sent them to Bethlehem and said, "Go and search carefully for the young Child, and when you have found Him, bring back word to me, that I may come and worship Him also." (Matthew 2:1–8)

We draw so much of what we think we know about these wise men, or Magi, from popular Christmas traditions. Storytellers have given them names, a song, matching outfits, camels, and a precise number: three. We don't know how many there were. It may have been nine—or nineteen. These men were essentially astrologers or wizards. They studied the heavens and then gave advice to their kings and rulers about what to do and which course to follow. In that sense, they were influential, highly respected, and very powerful. We call them "kings of the East," but in actuality they were more like the king makers. They influenced the king.

When they came into town, they were more than likely astride powerful Arabian horses (and certainly not camels). With their strange Eastern garb and long, conical hats, they certainly would have created a stir in Jerusalem. You didn't see guys like *that* ride into town every day.

If the appearance of these wise men created a stir, their repeated question created an even greater one: "Where is He who has been born King of the Jews?" Clearly, they weren't talking about Herod.

For his part, the highly paranoid Herod had his spies everywhere. The words *King of the Jews* must have struck him like a slap on the face. Why hadn't he been informed of this potential threat to his throne? That's why verse 3 reads, "When Herod the king heard this, he was troubled, and all Jerusalem with him." The word translated *troubled* here also could be rendered "to shake violently." Have you ever been around a washing machine when it gets out of balance and starts thumping loudly and lurching around? That was Herod in that moment. He was agitated, and in consequence, everyone was agitated. It's like that expression, "When Mama ain't happy, ain't nobody happy."

When Herod was angry, people around him were afraid—and for very good reason. They knew that heads were going to roll.

All of this may have given the dying, reprobate king a surge of new life. Now he had something to get up for in the morning—something to work on, something to do. With a potential threat to his throne out there, he had another person to find and kill. This time, it happened to be a baby.

The first people Herod called in were the clergy, the Jewish scribes and teachers who had made it their business to know the Scriptures.

"Do you guys know anything in the Scriptures about some king being born around here?"

What amazes me is that without missing a beat, they zeroed in on the right verse, Micah 5:2: "But you, Bethlehem Ephrathah, though you are little among the thousands of Judah, yet out of you shall come forth to Me the One to be Ruler in Israel, whose goings forth are from of old, from everlasting."

There was no question. The Messiah would be born in Bethlehem. Animated not only by his own hatred and paranoia, but also most likely driven by Satan himself, Herod then set out to destroy the Child before He could become a threat.

It's interesting to me to think about these Magi. These were pagan men, steeped in the occult, yet God came to them in a way they could readily understand: *through a special star.* In contrast, God sent angels to the shepherds out in the fields. They were good Jewish boys who believed in the Scriptures and knew about angels.

God reaches out to people in a million different ways, touching them and speaking to them in ways they understand. As the Lord told Jeremiah, "You will seek me and find me when you seek me with all your heart. I will be found by you" (Jeremiah 29:13–14, NIV). I believe that if a person is truly seeking God, no matter where he or she may be in this world, God will (somehow) reveal Himself to such a person. He will come to that individual in a way he or she understands. The way He touches the heart of a little child will not be the same way He moves in the soul of a teenager or creates a longing in the heart of a scientist.

He knows how to bring people to Himself. And sometimes He even gives you or me the privilege of being used by Him to touch someone's heart.

I'd like to add a note regarding the gifts the wise men brought to the Christ child. First, I'd like to point out that the gifts weren't wrapped. That's because these guys were *wise* men—and wise *men*. Most men I know don't like to wrap gifts. When I buy a gift for someone, the first question out of my mouth is, "Will you wrap this for me?" My son Christopher, however, was one of the best gift wrappers I have ever seen. He was meticulous, even to the point of creating hand-drawn wrapping paper and hand-drawn cards. So at least some men through the years have had this skill.

The wise men brought amazing gifts to the Child, including gold, frankincense, and myrrh. Each of the gifts spoke to an aspect of who this Child was and who He would be. They brought Him gold because He is a King. They brought Him incense because He would be our High Priest. And they brought Him myrrh, an embalming element, because He was destined to die for the sins of the world.

The wise men presented their gifts to a Child, not to a Baby, and they came to a house, not a stable. This obviously was a few months—even up to a couple of years—after the birth of our Lord.

God spoke to the wise men in a dream, warning them not to go back home through Jerusalem and certainly not to return to the evil Herod with information about the Child. Of course Herod was furious when he found out about it. And that is when the butcher of Bethlehem gave the order that all baby boys two years old or under living in the vicinity should be put to death.

Herod will have much to answer for when he stands before his Creator.

Let's take a moment to consider three primary individuals in this story. I think you will find yourself in one of the following three categories.

THREE CATEGORIES OF RESPONSES

1. There is Herod himself.

This is the man who tried to stop Christmas from ever taking place. In spite of his wealth, power, influence, title, and strategic connections, he came to complete ruin. In the final years of his life, his body was wasted by disease, with pain so great that he would scream through the night. According to commentator John MacArthur, the historian Joseph wrote that the wicked king died of "ulcerated entrails" with "putrefied and maggot-filled organs." He also suffered from "constant convulsions" and "neither physicians nor warm baths led to recovery."[1]

Herod ended up in the Dumpster of history, like dictators before and after him. It reminds us of other dictators on the world scene who fell from great power into a debased and disgraceful end. Hitler went down into his bunker and shot himself as his Third Reich crumbled around him. Saddam Hussein was found hiding in a hole and eventually was hung by his own people. Muammar Gaddafi was hunted down by his own people, beaten, and then shot to death. These cruel and evil rulers who lived such wicked lives eventually reaped what they sowed. They may blaspheme God, persecute His people, or try to stop the work of God for a while, but they eventually will fail. God's Word ultimately will prevail.

Herod wanted to be a big man, but he really was only a slave to his own corruption. He wanted to be known as "king of the Jews," but he became the king of fools.

Ironically, Herod pretended to be a worshiper. In Matthew 2:8 he told the Magi, "Go and search carefully for the young Child, and when you have found Him, bring back word to me, that I may come and worship Him also." Obviously, it was just talk. He had no intention of doing anything of the kind.

There are people like him today who say they believe in God but live lives that are a contradiction to everything the Scriptures teach. Jesus said, "Why do you call me, 'Lord, Lord,' and do not do what I say?" (Luke 6:46, NIV).

2. There are the religious scholars and scribes.

These men should have known better. They knew the Scriptures inside and out and were the top theological scholars of their day. It was the scribes' job to study the Scriptures and number the letters and the lines to ensure careful copying. Herod was right in expecting them to have an answer about where the Messiah would be born. And they knew the answer immediately.

Their response really puzzles me. They believed in God. They believed in the Scriptures. They knew what the prophet Micah said about where the Messiah would be born. They, too, had seen the mysterious visitors from the East who spoke of a star and a newborn King. Bethlehem was only about five miles from Jerusalem, a little more than an hour's walk.

Why didn't they go to see for themselves?

Was it all just dry and academic to them? Didn't they have any desire to see the One who could very well be Israel's Messiah?

Apparently not.

I think it was because they didn't care about a baby King; they wanted an adult monarch who could line their pockets with gold. It's not that they hated Jesus or saw Him as a threat. *They simply didn't care about Him.* They couldn't be bothered. They were too busy and wrapped up in their own little worlds to bother themselves over such things. They were "religious," but their hearts were ice-cold toward God.

As strange as it may sound, the biggest thing that will keep many people away from Christ is religion. When you seek to speak to them about a relationship with the Lord, they will say, "I already know that. I've already heard that. Don't waste your time."

Participating in the externals of religion without a living, vital relationship with Jesus can actually dull the spiritual senses to the Word of God and the voice of the Holy Spirit.

One sure way to get sleepy, of course, is to eat a lot of food. On Thanksgiving Day, for instance, we eat a lot of turkey and then go into a collective coma. Then we wake up and head for the kitchen to make turkey sandwiches! Sometimes it's like that when people are in a good, Bible-teaching church. They hear the truth over and over again, never put that truth into action, and fall into complacency. If we're not careful, if we don't take pains to stay alert, we can find ourselves spiritually asleep.

The New Testament warns against the dangers of this spiritual drowsiness and apathy. In the book of Ephesians we read, "Wake up, sleeper, rise from the dead, and Christ will shine on you" (5:14, NIV). Believers can fall asleep just like the religious scholars and scribes in Jesus' day—even to the point of knowing the truth but not really caring anything about it. They missed out on one of the greatest events in all of history. We can act in the same way if we "celebrate" the birth of Christ but never give our relationship with Him a passing thought.

3. There are the wise men.

As we've mentioned, these men were occultists, but God reached into their dark world with a star to bring them to their Creator. These were followers of the stars who met the Lord Jesus Christ who created the stars. Matthew 2:2 says, "We have seen His star in the East and have come to worship Him." And that's exactly what they did. Verse 11 says, "When they had come into the house, they saw the young Child with Mary His mother, and fell down and worshiped Him."

Everyone worships something at Christmas—it doesn't matter if they are Christians, atheists, skeptics, lawyers, or college professors. It may not be God whom they are worshiping, but they *are* worshiping. Some worship material things, which they never seem to have enough of. Others worship pleasure. Others worship their own bodies. Some might even worship their family. Another might worship some god of his own making.

Everyone worships at Christmas. The wise men showed themselves to be very wise indeed by worshiping Jesus Christ.

What does it mean to worship God? Christians toss that word around a lot. The word comes from the old English term *worthship.* It means to ascribe worth or value to something or someone. A god of our own making, however, isn't worthy of our worship. All of these lesser gods in our lives eventually will disappoint us and let us down. But the true and living God is worthy of our praise.

Two words are often used in the Scriptures to define worship. One means "to bow down and do homage." That speaks of reverence and respect. Another word, however, means "to kiss toward," which speaks of intimacy and friendship. Obviously, you would never kiss a stranger (unless you want to get slugged in the face). You would only kiss someone you are very close to. This is why it was such a despicable act for Judas to betray our Lord with a kiss. He turned what seemed to be an act of reverence and worship into a cruel, deceitful thing.

We come into God's presence, and we are in awe of Him. We respect and reverence Him, and at the same time there is a closeness and intimacy because of what Jesus has done to bring us into this relationship with the Father.

As Paul writes in Galatians, "But when the set time had fully come, God sent his Son, born of a woman, born under the law, to redeem those under the law, that we might receive adoption to sonship. Because you are his sons, God sent the Spirit of his Son into our hearts, the Spirit who calls out, 'Abba, Father' " (4:4–6, NIV).

How can we worship? One way, of course, is to sing His praises, right out loud. It's not the only way to worship, but it's certainly an important one. In fact, worshiping in song is something we will do both on Earth and in Heaven. Revelation 5:9 says of the residents of Heaven that "they sang a new song."

And what was the song they sang, with angels singing right alongside redeemed men and women?

Worthy is the Lamb, who was slain,
to receive power and wealth and wisdom and strength
and honor and glory and praise! (verse 12, NIV)

The fact is, however, that we don't always *feel* like worshiping, do we? This is why the book of Hebrews speaks of bringing a "sacrifice of praise" to the Lord (13:15). We should praise the Lord simply because He deserves it. The Bible doesn't say, "Give thanks unto the Lord because you feel good." It says, "Give thanks to the LORD, for He is good!" (Psalm 106:1). I praise Him because it is the right thing to do—not because I happen to be in the mood to do so.

When was the last time you said words like these to God? "Lord, I love You. I recognize all that You have done for me, and I thank You." If you love someone, you need to say so.

Of course there are other ways to worship as well. Serving others can be an act of worship. One of the ways the word *worship* is translated in the Scriptures carries the meaning of serving and ministering to others. In our Lord's encounter with the Devil in the wilderness, one of His replies to Satan was, "You shall worship the LORD your God, and Him only you shall serve" (Matthew 4:10). Why did Jesus say that? Because He understood that worship *leads* to service. Inevitably, you will end up serving whatever it is that you worship. As you make it a practice to worship God with all your heart, you will find yourself looking for opportunities to serve Him. Hebrews 13:16 reminds us, "Do not forget to do good and to share with others, for with such sacrifices God is pleased" (NIV).

Sometimes the simplest tasks done for others with Christ in mind become an act of worship to the Lord.

I think what we really long for at Christmas isn't the holiday, but it is Christ Himself. The fact is that you and I were designed by God to know Him and be with Him and walk with Him. You were designed—prewired when you emerged from the womb—to worship.

Let's do that with our songs, with our words of praise, and with willing hands that help and serve others . . . for the sake of the King.

10

WHAT THE SHEPHERDS FOUND

Now there were in the same country shepherds living out in the fields, keeping watch over their flock by night. And behold, an angel of the Lord stood before them, and the glory of the Lord shone around them, and they were greatly afraid. Then the angel said to them, "Do not be afraid, for behold, I bring you good tidings of great joy which will be to all people. For there is born to you this day in the city of David a Savior, who is Christ the Lord. And this will be the sign to you: You will find a Babe wrapped in swaddling cloths, lying in a manger."

And suddenly there was with the angel a multitude of the heavenly host praising God and saying:

"Glory to God in the highest,
And on earth peace, goodwill toward men!"

So it was, when the angels had gone away from them into heaven, that the shepherds said to one another, "Let us now go to Bethlehem and see this thing that has come to pass, which the Lord has made known to us." And they came with haste and found Mary and Joseph, and the Babe lying in a manger. Now when they had seen Him, they made widely known the saying which was told them concerning this Child. And all those who heard it marveled at those things which were told them by the shepherds. But Mary kept all these things and pondered them in her heart. Then the shepherds returned, glorifying and praising God for all the things that they had heard and seen, as it was told them.

(Luke 2:8–20)

The wise men, as we have noted, weren't anywhere around on the night when Jesus was born in that stable in Bethlehem. Most likely they were still back in their observatories in the mysterious East, studying their charts—and perhaps puzzling over the emergence of a strange new star.

The shepherds, however, were eyewitnesses to the events that night, undoubtedly the most remarkable night in history, when the Son of God was born as a tiny baby to a human mother.

As a group, the shepherds couldn't have been more different than the Magi. Where the wise men were at the top of the economic scale, the shepherds were at the bottom. In fact, these men were the lowest of the low in Jewish culture.

A shepherd was despised and mistrusted by the rest of society. They were thought to be crafty and dishonest, and they weren't allowed to observe the ceremonial hand washings of that day. The testimony of a shepherd wasn't even allowed in a court of law at that time. As men of the field, they smelled just like their work: sheep. The only people lower on the social ladder in Israel were those with leprosy.

Think of all the people to whom God might have brought this stunning message. The angels might have easily appeared in the court of Caesar himself. They could have burst into the court of King Herod with their glad tidings. They could have given the announcement to any number of political, military, or economic leaders of the day.

But God didn't send them to the rich, powerful, or influential.

It was as though He had said, "Who is the lowest of the low? Who are the ones that no one cares about? The shepherds. They are the ones to whom I will bring My message: 'There is born to you this day in the city of David a Savior, who is Christ the Lord.' "

The Lord came to the shepherds where they were, and He came to the Magi where they were.

WHAT WE LEARN FROM THE SHEPHERDS AND WISE MEN

1. God comes to us wherever we are.

Both the shepherds and the wise man received the announcement of Christ's birth. For the shepherds, it came with a stunning display in the heavens and a vast choir of angels declaring the glorious event. For the wise men, it began with the appearance of a mysterious star in the heavens that led them on a long journey to Bethlehem.

A number of years ago, an author named Robert S. McIvor wrote a book entitled *Star of Bethlehem, Star of Messiah*. In this book, McIvor cites records from ancient Chinese and Korean astronomers who recorded an unusual star appearing around the time of Christ's birth. In fact, according to the author, the appearance of a mysterious star was a worldwide event. Some scholars think the star may have been an appearance of the Shechinah glory of God.

Whatever the case, two revelations came to two groups of people, and they both believed God's Word.

At this point in history, there had been four hundred years of silence since the last biblical prophet had spoken. There had been no prophetic utterances, no angelic appearances, and no miracles performed.

And then, Heaven broke that silence. God Himself stepped back into human history with angelic appearances to Zacharias, the father of John the Baptist; to Mary, the mother of Jesus; and to Joseph, Mary's husband-to-be. Out in the distant East, He began directing the attention of the Magi to a mysterious sight in the heavens. And finally, on the night of Jesus' birth, the night sky suddenly was torn open, with angels unleashing a torrent of praise on a group of frightened shepherds.

The point is that God will come to you wherever you are. No one is beyond His reach.

The shepherds probably were raised in good Jewish homes where they learned about the God of Israel, the God of Abraham, Isaac, and Jacob. The very sheep they were raising may have been intended for temple sacrifices. If that were the case, they would have been very familiar with the need for animal sacrifice in approaching God under the Old Covenant.

You might have been raised in a Christian home, having had the privilege of hearing the Word of God since you were a little boy or a little girl. You have heard the name of Jesus as far back as you can remember.

But here is the problem. Sometimes a person who has grown up around Christianity all of his or her life can become more spiritually indifferent than a person who has not. You might be like some of the religious leaders in Israel at that time and know a great many things in your head, but you have no real relationship with God. You've heard the gospel so many times, and you say, "Yes, yes, I know all that. I've heard that. I don't want to talk about that." Don't let that happen to you. Don't let your heart get hardened toward God.

The wise men, on the other hand, were steeped in superstition, occultism, and false belief. God in no way condoned their pagan lifestyle, but He used a star to reach them, draw them, touch their hearts, and bring them to Himself. Wherever you are, God will reach you.

As I've mentioned, I wasn't raised in a Christian home, had never heard the Bible, and never went to church. But God invaded my world, and I responded to Him. He can invade yours as well.

Anyone who is truly seeking Him will find Him. In Jeremiah 29:13, the Lord says, "You will seek Me and find Me, if you search for Me with all your heart." If someone is deceived by a cult or a false belief—as the wise men were—I believe that if they really hunger to know God, He will reveal Himself to them.

That is the story of the whole Bible: it is a record of God revealing Himself to mankind. He is not a God who hides Himself; He wants men and women to know Him and draw near to Him. In the first chapters of Genesis, what we see is man hiding from God after he had sinned, not God hiding from man. In fact, God came looking for Adam and Eve, calling out, "Where are you?"

In the case of the Magi, God directed followers of the stars through a star that led them to Christ. In other words, He came to where they were to bring them to where they needed to be.

In the same way, we as Christians need to go with the gospel to where people are. Jesus didn't say that the whole world should go to church, but He did say that the church should go to the whole world. We need to be like one of those stars, so to speak, that would bring others to Christ. God can use you in that way.

Many follow the latest antics of the Hollywood celebrities. What are they up to now? What party are they going to? Who is dating whom and who is wearing what? God has zero interest in that. He sees a different kind of star. The person who is a star in God's eyes is the man or woman who will seek to bring others to faith. In fact, we are told over in the book of Daniel, "Men and women who have lived wisely and well will shine brilliantly, like the cloudless, star-strewn night skies. And those who put others on the right path to life will glow like stars forever" (12:3, MSG).

The shepherds and the wise men also worshiped the Lord. Those wise men would not let anything keep them away. Wild horses could not keep them away. In Luke 2:16, the New King James Version says, "They came with haste." Another version says, "They left, running" (MSG). They were sprinting. They wanted to see for themselves.

I am amazed at what will keep some people away from church: a drop of rain, a sniffle, waking up in a bad mood. And people will say, "You know, I just don't feel like going to church today. I'm staying home."

But look at what people will endure to go to a football game. I was watching a game on TV the other day where they were playing in a virtual blizzard. A guy would catch a pass and slide for ten feet. And the stands were full! There wasn't an empty seat, even in the snow and the wind chill. When they did close-ups of the fans in the stadium, they were screaming, yelling, jumping around, and had their faces painted with their team colors.

Yet people will say, "I can't go to church today. It just isn't convenient." And if they do go to church, and they lift their hands higher than their shoulders during worship, someone close to them will mutter, "Fanatic. That's embarrassing."

If only we would have as much passion for the Lord as some people have for their favorite athletic teams. We believers should have much more passion. What's a national championship? What's the Final Four? What's the World Series? What's the Superbowl? We have been given eternal salvation by our Lord and Savior, and we have the privilege of walking with Him and serving Him through all the days of our lives, until He takes us home. Now *that's* something to get excited about!

The Messiah has come. And His name is called Immanuel, *which means "God with us."*

It doesn't get any better than that.

2. We must respond to the call.

God came to both the wise men and the shepherds at different times and in different ways. But both groups of men had something in common. They *responded* to the call of God. The Magi, in their comfortable dwellings in the distant East, might have said, "Jerusalem? Are you kidding me? Do you know how far away that is? That could take weeks. And then when we get there, who knows what we'll find?"

It wasn't a matter of booking a flight or printing out a map from MapQuest and jumping into their SUVs. No, this was a very long journey, likely on horseback, with all sorts of hazards and trials along the way. But they went anyway. They wanted to see for themselves. Even though they were potentially sacrificing their own prestige and reputation to go to this unknown land, they made the trip, saying, "Where is He who has been born the King of the Jews? For we have . . . come to worship Him."

The shepherds might have stayed away, too. For them, it wasn't such a long journey, but they may very well have felt unworthy and unwanted. Most people didn't like shepherds or want them around.

What if they were rejected or turned away?

Have you ever gone someplace where you suddenly felt that people weren't glad to see you? You show up at the door, and people look up and then look away. The conversation stops, and the atmosphere suddenly feels awkward or uncomfortable. What a terrible feeling that is. And these shepherds, after all the rejection they had experienced through the years, might have said to each other, "Aw, what's the use? We're not dressed right. We don't know the right things to say. We don't know the protocol. Besides, they won't want us there. Nobody wants shepherds around."

The Bible says, "They came with haste and found Mary and Joseph, and the Babe lying in a manger" (Luke 2:16). One paraphrase says, "They ran to the village" (TLB). So they would have been out of breath when they arrived, with their hearts pounding.

They answered God's call quickly.

3. They believed and worshiped.

Both the Magi and the shepherds made a diligent search for Jesus. When the shepherds left the stable, the Bible says, "The shepherds went back to their flocks, glorifying and praising God for all they had heard and seen. It was just as the angel had told them" (Luke 2:20, NLT).

And as we noted earlier, the Magi actually fell down in the presence of the child Christ and worshiped Him.

What we see here is an eagerness to worship Christ. You'll hear many people talk about how Christmas has been ruined by crass commercialism or political correctness or by all the materialism and buying frenzy associated with it. We might even find ourselves saying that we dread the entire holiday.

While it's the truth that we can't do much about what Christmas has become in our culture, we can look at it through a different set of lenses. We can use it as a motivation to worship our Lord. We can emulate the eagerness of the shepherds to be in His presence. We can follow the example of the Magi who set their hearts to find Him and wouldn't be satisfied with anything less.

We can use this season of the year to thank Him for coming, to praise Him for being born on Earth so that He could grow up and die for our sins, opening the door to Heaven for us and giving us a reason and a purpose for living.

It's interesting to note that we are never commanded in the Scriptures to remember the birth of Jesus. No, there's nothing wrong with doing that; it is a good and worthy thing to do. But we are commanded in the Scriptures to remember His death. In that Upper Room with His disciples, before He went to the cross, Jesus said,

"Take, eat; this is My body which is broken for you; do this in remembrance of Me" (1 Corinthians 11:24).

He wants us to remember Him. He wants us to worship Him.

11

THE PROMISE OF CHRISTMAS

don't know about you, but I have always believed in the promise of Christmas.

There is something very special, wonderful, even magical (in the best sense of that word) about this time of year. My memories of Christmas go back to my earliest childhood and have grown through the years.

To this day, I feel a sense of wonder, beauty, and anticipation as Christmas approaches. I probably love the same things that you do: being with loved ones, eating incredible food, and watching for the excitement on a small child's face as he or she opens up a gift.

It is also a time that, for the most part, is marked by an absence of meanness. Yes, I know the stories of crazed people charging into stores and fighting over the latest electronic devices, and I have seen people almost go to war over parking places at the mall. But for the most part, people will show an extra measure of kindness at this time of year. You might find yourself talking to a person you wouldn't normally talk to. Why? Because it's Christmas, and you suddenly have a few things in common.

You might say Merry Christmas to a complete stranger on the street and get the same greeting back—or at least a weak Happy Holidays.

But here is the question: For all our anticipation of Christmas every year, does it really deliver on its promises?

Yes—sometimes—a little here and a little there. But for the most part, the holiday itself really doesn't deliver on all the hype and hoopla that surrounds it. What it does deliver is a lot of difficulty.

If you are a man, your blood pressure will go up dramatically during this time of year. I read a newspaper article by a British psychologist who found that shopping is actually hazardous for men's health. The article said they tested male volunteers aged 22 to 79 by sending them out Christmas shopping. The researchers recorded the fact that these volunteers' blood pressure shot up to levels that you would see "in a fighter pilot going into combat." When they did the same test on women, however, there was no change in their blood pressure at all. So I guess the ladies are just more suited for that kind of stress than we guys are.

CHRISTMAS LONGINGS

Ever since I was a little boy, I have believed in the promise of Christmas. I always wanted a *real* family Christmas. I would watch those programs on TV where the families would gather around the table and carve the turkey and give out the presents. But I never had a stable family growing up, with my mom being married and divorced so many times.

I remember one Christmas in particular where we were sitting around the tree. My mom was passed out from drinking too much. I recall looking at this fake, little white Christmas tree with one of those turning wheels and multicolored panes that continually changed the color of the tree. There was Christmas music playing in the background, but the room was permeated with the smell of stale smoke and alcohol. I thought to myself, even as a little boy, *It has got to get better than this.*

And it did!

It began when I was in high school, with receiving Jesus Christ as my Lord and Savior and stepping into a whole new life. But even before I became a Christian, I had determined that I would find the right woman, get married, *stay* married, and give my family a stable, loving home. I didn't want anyone to have to experience what I had experienced growing up in an unhappy, alcoholic home.

I also determined that when I had children, they would have a merry Christmas. God gave Cathe and me two boys, and I can tell you that it's the easiest thing in the world to buy toys for boys when you're a dad. It was never a challenge! I would see something and say, "Hey, this is cool. They will like it." And most of the time, I was right. Then, when

God gave Cathe and me granddaughters, it was like starting at square one. Buying for girls is a completely different experience.

Each year with my boys, I tried to top myself from the Christmas before, probably spending too much money and getting them elaborate gifts. I definitely was more excited than they were on Christmas mornings, wanting them to get up with me at the first light of dawn and see what I had given them. Most of the time they just wanted to sleep a little longer and open the presents at their leisure.

Then came 2008, the first Christmas after losing Christopher, my son of thirty-three years who died in a traffic accident in July of that year. Anyone who has lost a loved one will know what I mean when I say that the Christmas season is laced with emotional land mines. Memories can be triggered by a thousand different things: a song, a scent, a conversation, even someone's casual remark. A recollection seemingly pops up out of nowhere, and you're hit by a wave of pain.

CANCELING CHRISTMAS?

So after considering all of these things for a number of years, I have made a somewhat radical decision: I think we ought to cancel Christmas and make it official right now.

No, wait a minute. I guess I don't mean Christmas itself. I love Christmas. But I want to cancel what Christmas has *become* in our culture. I want to cancel this contemporary, generic version of "the holidays" that so many people buy into today.

Or, at the very least, I want to cancel it for myself.

No, I'm not saying that you have to unstring your lights or pitch out your Christmas tree or stop giving presents to one another. (I do, however, think I can make a pretty good case for removing fruitcake from the planet.)

What I am suggesting is that we cancel the hijacked version of Christmas. I think the very word *Christmas* has been pirated, emptied of its meaning, drained of its wonder, cheapened in its value, dragged through the gutter, and given back to us minus its beauty and power. Let's cancel the version of Christmas that is filled with hype and endless activity leading to exhaustion and that gives little to any thought of Christ. Let's cancel the Christmas where people bow to political correctness and take anything to do with Jesus right out of the picture. Let's cancel this artificial, counterfeit, commercial holiday we call Christmas or "the holidays" and instead celebrate the birth of Jesus Christ.

I still believe in the promise of Christmas—not in this holiday as we celebrate it for the most part. I still believe in the real message of Christmas, which is the birth of our Lord and the entrance of our God into time and space and a human body.

Due to our nation's faltering economy, I think many are bracing themselves for a tough Christmas. Because people aren't able to spend what they used to spend and do all they used to do, they tell themselves (with a sigh) that it won't be Christmas "like it used to be."

No, it may not be like it used to be. And that may be the best news yet. In fact, it may be better—much better.

What if it were a brighter, more peaceful Christmas than any you have ever experienced before? What if you were freed from the pressure of getting stuff from people and people getting stuff from you because you said, "Let's just forget about all that and be together and think about what all this really means"?

That could be a really good Christmas. It actually could be the best Christmas of your life. Why? Because the primary message of Christmas isn't "Let it snow" or "Let's shop till we drop." The real message is "Let us worship." That is what the wise men came to do. They said, "Where is He who has been born King of the Jews? For we have seen His star in the East and have come to worship Him" (Matthew 2:2).

And when they saw that star leading toward Bethlehem, the Scriptures say "they rejoiced with *exceedingly* great joy" (verse 10, emphasis added). The word *exceedingly* means "to the highest measure." The word *great* in the original language is *megas*, from which we get our word *mega* or *gigantic*.

RED

So let me do my own translation here: When the wise men knew for sure that God was directing them to Bethlehem where they would see the young King, they were megajoyful, with a happiness that went beyond all measure.

I think we can confidently say that these men had never been so joyful and excited in their entire lives.

They weren't going to see a Christmas lights display or listen to a Christmas concert or attend a Christmas drama, and they didn't have front-row tickets to some big Hollywood–Vegas-style extravaganza.

They were on their way to a simple little house in a tiny little village to see a little toddler who happened to be the King of kings.

It was the prospect of worship that sent their hearts soaring.

How long has it been since your heart soared like that? How long has it been since you have experienced sheer, mega, beyond-measure, over-the-top joy? When you got a new iPhone? Probably not. When your team scored a touchdown in a big bowl game? How long did that last?

It is worship that brings us deep-down, lasting joy. And no wonder. We were made to worship. It's in our DNA. It's part of our wiring.

Worship releases us from boredom.

Worship lifts our anxieties.

Worship melts away our fears.

Worship restores the sense of wonder we had as children.

This doesn't mean that all our circumstances will be perfect or that our lives will be a stroll through fields of daisies. Not at all. Every one of us will face hardships, challenges, and even tragedy. The Bible never teaches that we will have problem-free, pain-free, or sorrow-free lives as followers of Christ. But the Bible does teach that we never will be alone. And because of that, we don't have to be afraid.

Ray Stedman said that the chief mark of the Christian ought to be the absence of fear and the presence of joy. He wrote, "Authentic Christians operate by a belief in God's grace, love, and ultimate control."[1]

In Psalm 91:15 the Lord says to the believer, "I will be with him in trouble." Did you catch that? He doesn't say He will shield us *from* trouble; He says that He will be with us *in* trouble.

He will be *with us* in trouble. God will be with us. That's the whole meaning of the word *Immanuel*. And that's the very message that our weary, cynical, sin-sick world needs to hear.

If Christmas doesn't deliver for you, then it isn't really the fault of Christmas. It's our fault. We have built up this holiday so much in our minds that no single event ever could really achieve what we are anticipating.

Christmas can't bring harmony to your home.

Christmas can't bring peace on earth.

Christmas can't repair broken or strained relationships.

Christmas can't wash away your sins and regrets.

Christmas can't restore joy to a bitter, unhappy heart.

Christmas can't make you like a little child again.

That's the bad news. But the good news is that Christ Himself—the living Son of God—can do all of that and more. In fact, He can do anything. A holiday never can transform our lives, but Jesus both can and will. And that is what we are really longing for deep inside.

There really is a promise of Christmas, but it is only operative as the promise of Christ Himself.

Anything short of Christ ultimately will disappoint, but He never will.

A few years ago, I wrote in my blog about how difficult Christmas was after losing my son. One person wrote back to me, having also experienced some recent tragedies. He said,

Christmas continues to be bittersweet at times because of all the memories connected to it, and all the moments that will not be until we meet in Heaven one day. In a short time, I lost my father, mother, and two of my three brothers in unexpected and tragic ways—one through suicide. To say the least, Christmas has never been the same. And yet, as a believer, it is such a blessing and comfort to know that we find our hope in Him. And He will heal those sad places in our hearts. Listening to other believers share their story ministers to all of us. I can honestly say I have never felt more loved and comforted by the Lord than in this season through His Word, worship, teaching, and the encouragement of other believers.

This is a person who understands that while the Christmas of our contemporary culture may be hollow, the reality of Immanuel is a mighty truth, a powerful river of hope, deeper than the deepest pain, and as enduring as eternity. It is *God with us* that gives grieving souls the strength to go through what they are facing right now.

Before we leave this subject of the promise of Christmas, let's go back again to that incredible night—possibly the greatest, most amazing night in the history of our poor world—when a host of heavenly angels made that dramatic announcement to a motley crew of startled shepherds, out in the fields with their flocks.

Since many of us are so familiar with the words and the story, let's read it from a more contemporary version.

THE ANGELS AND THE PROMISE OF CHRISTMAS

There were sheepherders camping in the neighborhood. They had set night watches over their sheep. Suddenly, God's angel stood among them and God's glory blazed around them. They were terrified. The angel said, "Don't be afraid. I'm here to announce a great and joyful event that is meant for everybody, worldwide: A Savior has just been born in David's town, a Savior who is Messiah and Master. This is what you're to look for: a baby wrapped in a blanket and lying in a manger."

At once the angel was joined by a huge angelic choir singing God's praises:

Glory to God in the heavenly heights,
Peace to all men and women on earth who
    please him.

As the angel choir withdrew into heaven, the sheepherders talked it over. "Let's get over to Bethlehem as fast as we can and see for ourselves what God has revealed to us." They left, running, and found Mary and Joseph, and the baby lying in the manger. Seeing was believing. They told everyone they met what the angels had said about this child. All who heard the sheepherders were impressed. (Luke 2:8–18, MSG)

This version gives us a little different picture of that night. I've always visualized an event up in the sky somewhere, with the shepherds craning their necks to see—as though it were a fireworks display or an appearance of the aurora borealis. But in this text we read that the angel suddenly "stood among them and God's glory blazed around them."

Boom! Suddenly there was an angel standing there in front of them, blazing white-hot like a lightning bolt. They must have shielded their eyes. And then, after his brief announcement, their whole world exploded in beautiful, heavenly light, and that lonely field out in the hills was instantly filled with an army of celestial beings singing God's praises.

It was an illustration of what had already happened. Heaven had come to Earth. In that moment, Earth and Heaven were joined.

The shepherds were given a glimpse into eternal glory, and just for a moment, they were privileged to see how Heaven itself celebrates Christmas.

What was the hallmark of it all? It was *worship* . . . singing God's praises . . . declaring God's wonders . . . a Niagara Falls of joy falling over them, sweeping them away in its current.

By the way, Christmas in Heaven is way better than Christmas on Earth. I mentioned earlier how difficult it was in 2008 for us to celebrate our first Christmas without Christopher. But then the thought occurred to me. December 25, 2008, also was Christopher's first Christmas in Heaven. Down on Earth, we had the privilege of praising a Savior we've never seen. On the other side, Christopher was praising the Savior in His immediate presence! So who should have been feeling sorry for whom?

Through the years, ever since Christopher was born, I have been so preprogrammed to shop for him at this time of year. It was hard to stop, even when he had left for Heaven. I remember being in a store and seeing a shirt and thinking, *Oh, that shirt would be perfect for Topher. That's what I would get him if he were still here.*

I would have already known what he wanted because he always told me. Criticize me if you'd like, but I always tell my family, "Just tell me exactly what you want, and I will get it for you." And he always was happy to do that, even e-mailing me a link on my computer that would send me to a website and the exact item he wanted.

I don't know how long this will go on, but when I see something really cool in a store, I still find myself thinking, *Oh, I wish Christopher were here. I wish he could see this.* And then I wonder if he is thinking the same thing about me in Heaven. *I wish Dad could be up here to see this. This would blow him away.*

I try to picture those things, but it isn't easy. As the music group Mercy Me sings, "I can only imagine."

In Heaven it is pure bliss. There are no twinkling lights on a tree, but there's the radiant light of the Creator of light. There are no painted, metal angels on display, but there are the living, joyful, powerful, holy angels of God.

On Earth we have war and constant strife; in Heaven there is perfect harmony and peace. On Earth there is constant friction between family and friends; in Heaven there is feasting and perfect, unspoiled, unshadowed fellowship.

C. S. Lewis put it this way: "All the things that have ever deeply possessed your soul have been but hints of [Heaven]—tantalizing glimpses, promises never quite fulfilled, echoes that died away just as they caught your ear. . . . It is the secret signature of each soul, the incommunicable and unappeasable want."[2]

The splendor and magnificence of Heaven came to Earth on that night when the angels stepped through the curtain to appear to the shepherds. Though we may never experience that same event, something supernatural happens when we worship Jesus Christ. We put our minds on Heaven, and in some way that exceeds our understanding, we actually occupy the same ground as

Heaven. Listen to how Paul described it to the church at Colosse:

> Since you became alive again, so to speak, when Christ arose from the dead, now set your sights on the rich treasures and joys of heaven where he sits beside God in the place of honor and power. Let heaven fill your thoughts; don't spend your time worrying about things down here. (Colossians 3:1–2, TLB)

In other words, set your mind on Jesus Christ and the joys of Heaven, and some of that joy will touch your life here on Earth.

What, then, was the essence of the angel's message that night to the shepherds?

THE ANGELIC MESSAGE

1. Don't be afraid.

The angel said, "Don't be afraid" (Luke 2:10, MSG).

We read those words, but there is a lot to be afraid of today, isn't there? We're afraid of the future. We're afraid of terrorism. We're afraid of what's happening in our economy. We're afraid for our nation so obviously going into decline. We're afraid of what's going on in popular culture with depravity and twisted values becoming more and more mainstream. We're afraid for our families in such a debased, degraded culture. We're afraid of rogue nations using nuclear weapons against us. We're afraid for our marriages with all the stresses and strains that seek to tear us apart. We're afraid for the world our little grandchildren are coming into, the dark world within which they will have to navigate.

There is so much to be afraid of. But the angel said, "Don't be afraid."

Did you know that in the Bible, the phrase *don't be afraid* is used 365 times? That means there is one *don't be afraid* for every day of the year. Fear always will rob us of joy. It's hard to be afraid when you are joyful, and it is hard to be joyful when you are afraid.

A friend recently told me about his experience in a worship service. As the music was soaring and people around him were lifting their hands in praise, the Lord spoke to his heart and said, "You *can't* worship Me. Your insides are completely frozen with fear. Let Me deal with your fear, and then you will be able to praise Me." So that's just what he did. He released those fears to the Lord and felt them melt away in that time of worship. And then he could really worship the Lord and not just go through the motions.

So . . . don't be afraid. And why?

2. The Messiah has come.

"A Savior has just been born in David's town, a Savior who is

Messiah and Master" (Luke 2:11, MSG).

Why should the shepherds let go of their fear? Because Jesus had come. The Messiah had come. And He is the answer to every fear, no matter what it might be.

The angel was saying, "Your prayers are answered. The Messiah has come. He is going to go live a perfect life, and He will voluntarily die on a cross and bear your sins and the sins of the world. He will bodily rise from the dead three days later and ascend to Heaven as your representative and advocate before the throne of God."

And from our point of view, the Messiah not only has come, but He is *coming*. He will return to Earth, first for His church and then to rule and reign on Earth and set everything right once again.

Do you ever wonder about your future? *That* is your future—to rule and reign alongside King Jesus forever.

3. Because the Messiah has come—and will come again— rejoice!

"I'm here to announce a great and joyful event that is meant for everybody, worldwide" (Luke 2:10, MSG).

There is so much to be joyful for at this time of year that has nothing whatsoever to do with politics, the economy, the stock market, or what gifts await you under the Christmas tree.

There always will be trouble in our lives. We always will be dealing with *something*. You know that by now, don't you? If you're not going through some kind of a difficulty, either you are not breathing or you are in major denial. We all have problems in life. Don't feel as though you're the exception—*but rejoice anyway.*

You say, "I'll rejoice when I get through this trial."

No. Rejoice when you are *in* the trial. In fact, you are commanded to do so. In Philippians 4:4, the apostle Paul says, "Rejoice in the Lord always. Again I will say, rejoice!" In the original language, it is neither a suggestion nor a pleasant devotional thought. It is a command.

By the way, when Paul penned those words, He wasn't lying on some beach, sipping an iced tea with a tiny umbrella in the glass. He wasn't sitting in some ivory tower and spinning off theories. These words were written by a man who knew hardship as few of us ever will know it. He was a man who had a lot to potentially worry about.

When he actually wrote those words to the Philippians, he had nothing in his circumstances to rejoice about. He had wanted to go to Rome to preach, but instead he was there as a prisoner. Now, as a man in prison, he waited for his case to come up and for his fate. There was a chance that he might be acquitted. Then again, there was an equal chance that he might be beheaded—or boiled in oil. In Rome you never really knew for sure.

Besides that, there were some Christian brothers who had turned against him. Close friends had become enemies, beginning a whispering campaign against the apostle while he was in prison and couldn't defend himself. But even in the midst of such bleak circumstances, Paul said to the Philippians (and to all of us), "I have a message for you. *Lighten up!* Rejoice in the Lord always." In other words, he's saying, "If anyone has reason to be depressed, it is me. But I am *not* depressed. And you don't have to be, either."

The key element in finding joy is spending time in God's presence.

In the Psalms we are told, "In Your presence is fullness of joy" (Psalm 16:11). Another version reads, "You have let me experience the joys of life and the exquisite pleasures of your own eternal presence" (TLB).

And by the way, did you know that being joyful is good for your health? We are told in Proverbs 15:13, "A happy heart makes the face cheerful, but heartache crushes the spirit" (NIV). And Proverbs 17:22 says, "A cheerful heart is good medicine, but a broken spirit saps a person's strength" (NLT).

Am I suggesting here that you walk around with a fake smile plastered on your face, saying praise the Lord under your breath 24/7? No, I'm not. In fact, there is a place for sorrow, a place for mourning, a place for tears. We can acknowledge our heartaches and disappointments just like anyone else. But underneath it all, like two mighty underground rivers, there can be joy and hope. And that inner confidence eventually will bubble its way to the surface, even in the darkest of times.

This is such a powerful magnet to the nonbeliever. When a Christian can genuinely and authentically rejoice during times of suffering and pain, it is a powerful testimony for Jesus Christ.

Friedrich Nietzsche, the atheist and German philosopher, once said to some Christians, "If you want me to believe in your Redeemer, you're going to have to look more redeemed." And a lot of Christians don't look redeemed at all; they have a sour disposition—as though they had been baptized in lemon juice rather than in water. Do you look redeemed?

You might say, "But Greg, you really don't understand. I'm having a hard time this Christmas. There are problems in my life, problems in my marriage, problems with my kids, and problems with my health. My finances are in trouble. My best friend has turned against me. How can I rejoice in Christmas?"

I understand that. But I'm not talking about rejoicing *in Christmas*. I am talking about rejoicing *in Christ*. Christ has come. That is how we can have joy.

One of the most beautiful songs we hear at this time of year is "I Heard the Bells on Christmas Day," written by the American poet Henry Wadsworth Longfellow. The story behind it is very compelling.

In 1860 Longfellow was at the peak of his success as a poet, known and celebrated throughout the nation. There was a buoyant optimism in the air as Abraham Lincoln was elected to the presidency in November of that year, giving hope to many. In a matter of months, however, things turned very dark—both for the young nation and for Longfellow personally.

The Civil War began the next year, with the sickening prospect of brothers fighting against brothers and even fathers against sons. It was our country's greatest trial. And then to add to that, Longfellow faced a great personal tragedy: His wife was burned to death in a tragic accident in their home. In his attempt to save her, he, too, was severely burned. In fact, he was so badly hurt that he wasn't even able to attend her funeral. In his diary for Christmas, 1861, he wrote, "How inexpressibly sad are the holidays."

The following year, the toll of the war dead began to mount in a ghastly, almost incomprehensible way. On Christmas of that year Longfellow wrote, " 'A Merry Christmas,' say the children. There is no more for me." His son had run away unexpectedly and joined the army—only to be returned home with severe wounds.

That following Christmas, in 1863, things were so bleak that the great poet put no entry at all in his diary. Nevertheless, he wanted to pull out of his despair. So he tried to capture the joy of the season in verse. That poem became a familiar Christmas song for generations. He began it like this:

I heard the bells on Christmas Day
Their old, familiar carols play,
 And wild and sweet
 The words repeat
Of peace on earth, good-will to men!

But then he stopped and thought about the condition of his country. The terrible Battle of Gettysburg had recently occurred, and things were looking so dark. Longfellow wondered how he could write about the joy of the season. And then he continued on:

And in despair I bowed my head;
"There is no peace on earth," I said;
 "For hate is strong,
 And mocks the song
Of peace on earth, good-will to men!"

But then Longfellow, catching an eternal perspective, began to see his life and circumstances from God's point of view, leading him to conclude:

Then pealed the bells more loud and deep:
"God is not dead; nor doth He sleep!
 The Wrong shall fail,

> The Right prevail,
>
> With peace on earth, good-will to men!"[3]

We have got to get our perspective right. Mankind *never* will bring peace on earth. The United Nations *never* will persuade nations to agree with one another or stop fighting. You can "visualize world peace" all you'd like, but it will never occur until the Prince of Peace Himself takes His rightful throne. Don't buy into the utopian dream of anyone or anything—any politician, any political philosophy, any political party—bringing peace. We never will see real justice and lasting peace until Christ Himself comes back and establishes His kingdom on Earth.

That doesn't mean we shouldn't hope for peace or work for peace or pray for peace. But it does mean that we need to be realistic in our expectations. As long as human beings are in charge, there always will be friction and conflict.

The promise of Christmas is no promise at all apart from the Christ of Christmas.

WHAT YOU DON'T HAVE . . . AND WHAT YOU DO

There may be some things you wish you had that you don't have this Christmas. You may not have the resources to give what you would like to give to your loved ones and friends. You may be struggling with some physical problem and have ongoing pain that keeps you on the edge of discouragement and distress. You may be hurting over a broken relationship. You may have a loved one who was with you last year but won't be with you this year.

Those are things you don't have. But let me tell you about the things you *do* have.

Look back at Luke 2:11: "For there is born to you this day in the city of David a Savior, who is Christ the Lord." The fact is that you have a Savior, you have a Christ, and you have a Lord.

So don't look to Christmas—the holiday, the square on the calendar—to meet your expectations or fulfill your longings or bring you fulfillment. Look to Christ.

The truth is that we feel let down and disappointed because of false expectations as to what Christmas should be.

Some people don't mind taking time off to commemorate the birth of Jesus, but that's the extent of it. He is all right as long as He stays in that manger as a baby. They don't like the idea of Jesus growing into a man and dying on a cross for them and rising from the dead and telling them to turn from their sins.

There are many people who say, "I'm okay with God as long as He stays out of my life." They might have a bumper sticker on their car that says GOD IS MY COPILOT. That's nice. But the fact of the matter is they shouldn't even be in the cockpit. God doesn't want to be our copilot; He wants to be in control of our lives.

But that's where people want God. They want Him there in case of emergency, and that's about the extent of their faith. These people wrongly think they make their own luck and are the captains of their own ships, the masters of their own destinies.

ESCAPING THE TRAP

Some look down on Christians and say, "You people are a bunch of automatons, marching in lockstep. You want to do the will of God? Well, fine. But I want to do the will of me. *I'm* in control of my own life. *I* decide what direction I am going to take."

I have news for them: life doesn't work that way.

People who reject Jesus Christ are not in control of their own lives. Nor are they making their own luck. According to the Bible, those outside of Christ are under the control of someone else. And that someone else is known as Satan. In 2 Timothy 2:25–26, Paul writes this to believers:

> Be humble when you are trying to teach those who are mixed up concerning the truth. For if you talk meekly and courteously to them, they are more likely, with God's help, to turn away from their wrong ideas and believe what is true. *Then they will come to their*

senses and escape from Satan's trap of slavery to sin, which he uses to catch them whenever he likes, and then they can begin doing the will of God. (TLB, emphasis added)

You don't realize this when you're a nonbeliever. You imagine yourself to be in charge of your own life. You convince yourself that you're calling all the shots. But it's strange. Have you ever noticed how most nonbelievers do the same things? They get caught up in the same miserable lifestyle. And then one day, by God's grace, they wake up and look around and say, "What is this? What am I doing here? How did I get to this place? I hate this life."

That's what happened in Jesus' story of the lost son. This was the young man who took his share of his dad's inheritance, left for Vegas (or something like that), blew all his money, and ended up as a farm laborer feeding pigs in a pigpen. As he was watching the fat hogs grub around in the muck for scraps, he found himself thinking that some of those scraps were looking pretty good.

That's when it hit him. The Bible says, "He came to himself." And then he said, "I will arise and go to my father" (see Luke 15:11–32).

That's what happened to me, too, as a young man. I started looking around at my life and thought, *This stinks. I'm sick of these stupid parties. I'm tired of drinking and drugs. I can't stand all of these cliques and the way these people live. I've had enough of all the backstabbing and hypocrisy. There has to be something better.*

Those thoughts, that inner restlessness and dissatisfaction, sent me on a quest to find purpose and meaning. I thought, *Surely there's more to life than this.* The adult world that I'd been exposed to certainly wasn't the world where I wanted to live. The empty, unhappy lives of my friends and peers didn't appeal to me either.

So I started looking. My search led me to hearing the gospel and giving my life to Christ. Then I started going to church and hanging out with God's people, and I began seeing the reality I had been searching for all along, a place where love and brotherhood and joy could be experienced—not because you were high on something, but through a relationship with God.

Jesus filled all the longings in my life that I thought could never be filled.

He's still in the business of doing that.

He, and He alone, is the real promise of Christmas.

12

CHRISTMAS, THE MAIN EVENT

I heard about a wife who told her husband, "Honey, last night I dreamed this wonderful dream."

"And what did you dream?" he asked.

"Well, in my dream you gave me a *diamond necklace* for Christmas. It was so *beautiful*. It made me so happy! What do you think that means?"

"Hmm," he replied. "I guess you'll have to wait until Christmas Eve to find out."

She liked that answer and thought she knew what it meant. When the big night arrived, she could hardly contain her excitement. He came out with a beautifully wrapped box and placed it in her hands. Trembling with anticipation, she opened the box and found . . . a book entitled *The Meaning of Dreams*.

That is what you call a letdown, isn't it?

And that is the situation in which we find ourselves when we get our focus on gifts and shopping and expectations and trying so hard to please one another. We end up becoming distracted from the most amazing gift in the universe: the gift of God's Son.

Let's go back to the timeless story in the book of Luke and to a couple of paragraphs that we've considered a few times already in the pages of this book. Just for a few moments, let's allow the words to wash away all of the tensions and distractions and demanding voices that we encounter at this time of year.

> And it came to pass in those days that a decree went out from Caesar Augustus that all the world should be registered. This census first took place while Quirinius was governing Syria. So all went to be registered, everyone to his own city.
>
> Joseph also went up from Galilee, out of the city of Nazareth, into Judea, to the city of David, which is called Bethlehem, because he was of the house and lineage of David, to be registered with Mary, his betrothed wife, who was with child. So it was, that while they were there, the days were completed for her to be delivered. And she brought forth her firstborn Son, and wrapped Him in swaddling cloths, and laid Him in a manger, because there was no room for them in the inn. (2:1–7)

LUKE, THE REPORTER

Dr. Luke, the author of this gospel, was very meticulous in his reporting. He had a sharp mind and a sharp pencil, and though his gospel has an unmistakable poetic style, he was a stickler for the facts. As you may recall, Luke was not an eyewitness to the life of Jesus, as were Matthew and John, who also penned gospel accounts. He was a physician from a non-Jewish family and came to faith. His great desire was to write an accurate historical record of the life of Jesus. To do so, he most likely relied on interviews with the men and women who had known Jesus and walked with Him during His time on Earth.

I can imagine him sitting very respectfully with Mary, the mother of Jesus, and asking her, "Okay, Mary, let's go back to that day when Gabriel came to you in Nazareth. Exactly what did he say?" And he would have written this account on parchment. Then he would have tracked down some of the shepherds who had been watching over their flocks outside of Bethlehem on the night when Jesus was born. I can imagine that he interviewed every shepherd he could locate, asking them, "What was it like on that night? Can you describe that angelic chorus that appeared to you? What do you remember about locating the stable and finding the baby in the manger?"

In Luke 1:3 he stated that he was producing "an orderly account." Another way to translate that phrase would be "an exact account." In *The Message* version we read, "Since I have investigated all the reports in close detail, starting from the story's beginning, I decided to write it all out for you . . . so you can know beyond the shadow of a doubt the reliability of what you were taught" (verses 3–4).

We see an example of that orderly reporting in Luke 2:1–2. He places the events in a precise timeframe when he says that Caesar Augustus was emperor and that Quirinius was ruling over Syria.

Augustus was the first real Roman emperor. His original name was Gaius Octavius, and he was the great-nephew of Julius Caesar. Octavius was a born fighter who clawed his way to power by defeating Mark Antony and Cleopatra. The Roman Republic became the Roman Empire, the most powerful nation on the face of the earth. Rome had bludgeoned all other nations into submission, establishing what came to be known as the Pax Romana, or "Roman peace."

It was peace, all right—but it was peace at the end of a spear. All the world bowed before Rome, and Gaius Octavius was Caesar.

Julius Caesar had been the first Caesar, and that was his actual name. All the others who followed after him took the name Caesar as a title, which was just what Octavius did. But then he decided to add another name to his title and became Caesar *Augustus*. Augustus means "of the god."

In other words, this was the first Caesar to claim that he was a living god, a deity, whom people needed to worship. His predecessor, Julius Caesar, had claimed to be "the savior of the whole world," and now Octavius upped the ante by declaring himself divine.

This sheds a little light on something the angel said to the shepherds who were out in the fields at night, watching over their flocks. Luke records his words: "For there is born to you this day in the city of David a Savior, who is Christ the Lord. And this will be the sign to you: You will find a Babe wrapped in swaddling cloths, lying in a manger" (Luke 2:11–12).

A Savior, who is Christ the Lord . . . In other words, "Julius Caesar and Caesar Augustus are not saviors and are not divine. The real Savior of the world does not rule from Rome. In fact, He is lying in a feeding trough in a cave-stable in Bethlehem. This is the *real* Savior and Lord of the world."

RICHES TO RAGS

Jesus does not have what we would commonly call a rags-to-riches story. In fact, it was the other way around.

This is a riches-to-rags story. He went from unimaginable glory and power and splendor to a place of complete humility: an infant child born to poor parents in a conquered, subjected nation. He went from the magnificence of Heaven to a crude stable for animals.

I read once that when Queen Elizabeth last visited the United States, she brought five thousand pounds of clothing with her. By my calculations, that is two and a half tons. (Come to think of it, I don't think the airline charged her any extra for it, either.) She had two personal valets and a hairdresser on board as well, not to mention that the queen always has special leather covers for any toilet seats she would use. By anybody's standards, that is *not* traveling light.

Now, consider the ultimate Sovereign of the universe when He came to us. He was the King of kings, but He left everything behind.

Caesar might have thought he was in charge and a pretty big deal, calling himself "Caesar of the gods." He sent out a decree that all the world should be taxed, and because of that, everyone had to return to their hometowns to be registered. From an earthly perspective, then, the ruler in Rome imagined himself a demigod and could send out orders across the known world.

But he had it all wrong. Caesar was just a pawn in the hand of God Almighty. It reminds us that caesars and pharaohs, emperors and kings, prime ministers, dictators, and presidents come and go on the world stage. They make their little appearance, take a short bow, and then they are gone. But God is ultimately in control. The Alpha and the Omega is the One who really calls the shots. Even King Solomon realized this. In Proverbs 21:1 he wrote, "The king's heart is like a stream of water directed by the Lord; he guides it wherever he pleases" (NLT). In other words, God takes a little man who is big in his own mind and directs him as easily as you would turn a little rivulet of water with your pinkie finger.

We probably wouldn't even know the names of Quirinius or Caesar Augustus if they hadn't appeared as bit players in the story of Jesus Christ. They would have been forgotten. But because they were in power when Jesus was born, we remember them. Caesar Augustus may have been the most powerful man on the face of the earth at that time, but he is little more than a footnote in the greatest story ever told.

Now we greet his name with a shrug or a yawn. We say, "Who is this Caesar guy? Didn't they name a salad after him?" It reminds us that history truly is *His story*. And the fact is, the history of all humanity swings on the hinge of a stable door in Bethlehem.

So then, because of Caesar's decree, Joseph and Mary were on their way to Bethlehem. Did they have any idea at the time that they were fulfilling Bible prophecy? I doubt it. If that had been the case, I think they would have made the trip a little bit sooner and not in the ninth month of Mary's pregnancy. I don't think either one of them understood that God was directing their steps as they made that difficult journey.

When they finally arrived in Bethlehem, they had a rude awakening: no accommodations, no room for them in the inn, no place for their little one to be born as Mary's birth pangs began. In fact, this was a foretaste of the treatment Jesus would receive throughout His later ministry. There is a telling passage in the gospel of John where it says that "everyone went to his own house. But Jesus went to the Mount of Olives" (7:53–8:1).

Jesus spent a lot of time on the Mount of Olives, near Jerusalem, sleeping in the open air. As our Lord told one would-be follower, "Foxes have holes and birds of the air have nests, but the Son of Man has nowhere to lay His head" (Matthew 8:20).

There was no room in the inn. It seems like the only place there ever was room for Jesus was on a cross. The Lord had told His disciples, "In My Father's house are many mansions. . . . I go to prepare a place for you" (John 14:2). So we human beings don't have any room for Him, but He has plenty of room for us.

SEPARATING TRUTH FROM EMBELLISHMENT

Going back to this innkeeper in the Christmas story . . . everyone talks about an innkeeper, and he shows up in the numerous Christmas pageants and stories. But the Bible doesn't mention such a person at all. It simply records the fact there was no room for Mary and Joseph when they arrived.

Speaking of Mary, in all the religious art or in movie depictions of her, she is always dressed in blue. Everyone else might be in rags, but Mary comes into the scene swathed in blue and riding on a donkey. Of course, you can't miss her anyway because she and Joseph are usually pictured with halos around their heads.

But there is nothing about a blue garment in the Bible, nothing about halos, and for that matter, nothing about a donkey. We assume there was a donkey, but the hard truth is that Mary may have had to walk. Of course we can be pretty sure she was very young—perhaps as young as twelve but certainly not older than fourteen. If anyone had noticed them at all, they would have looked just like any other poor young couple among the crowds, arriving to register and pay their tax.

Joseph was likely young too. If they did approach an innkeeper, what he would have seen were two impoverished young people dressed in ragged clothing, soiled from the journey—and one of them a very pregnant girl. By the way, when you think of the inn, don't think of a Holiday Inn or a Best Western. Some of the better places in that place and time might have had a roof and a fire and some food, but the more primitive inns simply would be enclosures—four walls where you could bring yourself and your animals in off the street. In that more common sort of inn, there would have been no room and no food. But Joseph and Mary couldn't even get a spot within the walls. Because there was nowhere else for them to go, someone offered them the use of a cave out back somewhere, with the animals.

So was this nameless individual who offered Joseph and Mary room in a stable out back behind the inn a heartless villain, as he is so often portrayed? Not really. He's just like a lot of people around us every day—people so preoccupied with their jobs and lives and families and pursuits that they don't have any time or room for God. Ironically, this state of mind can become even more pronounced at Christmastime. People rush around shopping and going to parties and hurrying here and there. Someone once said you could write on the tombstone of many Americans, "Hurried, worried, buried."

We can be so busy that we don't have time for God. We don't carve out time to pray or read and think about His Word or get together with other believers in church to worship Him. Life is "too hectic."

So we don't have room for Him in our inns, either.

The stable

We have all seen romanticized versions of the stable—especially in our Nativity scenes. As I have indicated already, it may have been nothing more than a cave—cold, damp, and very dark. You sometimes hear about babies being born in the back seat of a car or taxi cab, but those places would be much more desirable than a dirty animal stable, filled with straw and animal manure. God incarnate was born on the dirt floor of a filthy cave.

So it wasn't like the pictures we've seen or the depictions represented on Christmas cards with fresh golden straw, happy animals looking on, and a stable flooded with heavenly light. Does this make me appreciate the scene less? Not at all. In fact, I appreciate it more when I think of the sacrifice Jesus made to leave Heaven and to come to us.

Commentator R. Kent Hughes wrote these words: "It was a leap down—as if the Son of God rose from His splendor, stood poised on the rim of the universe, and dove headlong, speeding through stars over the Milky Way to earth's galaxy, . . . where he plunged into a huddle of animals. Nothing could be lower."[1]

He came as a fertilized egg. And then the One who was larger than the whole universe became a human embryo . . . a fetus . . . and finally a little baby.

Babies are so amazing. I remember holding my little grandson Christopher in my arms and just looking at him when he was just six or seven months old. At that point, he was beginning to look around, responding to faces and voices. I started singing some Christmas carols to him, and he looked right at me. No one else in the room may have appreciated my singing, but Christopher did. You have to be gentle and careful with babies. They're completely helpless. What a wonder that God would humble Himself in such a way!

G. K. Chesterton wrote, "The hands that had made the sun and stars were too small to reach the huge heads of the cattle."[2]

Augustine described Him as "unspeakably wise, wisely speechless; filling the whole world, lying in a manger; . . . though insignificant in the form of man, so great in the form of God."[3]

He was a true baby thinking baby thoughts. He was God, but He had deliberately veiled His deity rather than voiding it.

Mary and Joseph wrapped the baby in rags. That's basically what "swaddling cloths" are. This symbolized His whole life on Earth, from the cradle to the cross. He could have been born in the most elegant mansion on the ritziest boulevard in Rome. He could have had aristocratic parents. He could have had the finest clothes from the most exclusive shops. He could have had legions of angels as an army of servants to respond to His whims. But He laid all of that aside for us. As Paul wrote in 2 Corinthians 8:9, "You know how full of love and kindness our Lord Jesus was: though he was so very rich, yet to help you he became so very poor, so that by being poor he could make you rich" (TLB).

The baby announcement

So God's Son has been born on Earth. Who would be the first

to get the news? Whom would He tell?

If you have ever had a child, you can probably remember who got the first phone call with the news. You may have called your mom or dad, a brother or sister, or maybe some close friends. You would have said, "It's a boy!" or "It's a girl!" and then gave the baby's weight. If you sent out birth announcements, you would have included the day and perhaps even the hour when the baby entered the world.

But whom did God call? Whom did God tell?

The logical thing would have been to have the angel Gabriel appear right in front of Caesar Augustus and his royal court. Or He might have announced the birth to the Sanhedrin, the religious and political leaders in Jerusalem. He could have sent His angel to them with the message, "Hey you, leaders, wake up! The Messiah has come—the One you always talk about and pray for! Well, guess what? He's here!"

But no, God chose to announce the royal birth to . . . shepherds. They were the very first to get the word. Heaven chose to honor them in a remarkable way, and we're still talking about it and singing about it two millennia later.

Through the years we have come to prettify and idealize these shepherds along with all the other elements of the Christmas story. But the truth is that shepherds were at the bottom of the social ladder. They were rejected and despised people. In fact, the testimony of a shepherd wasn't even allowed in a court of law. Why? Because it was just assumed they would lie.

In today's world the announcement might have read, "Now there were certain used car salesmen watching over their lots by night" or maybe, "There were certain telemarketers calling people in the night, and an angel appeared to them."

Shepherds did the work that no one else wanted to do. They were hardworking men with dirt under their fingernails—rednecks, if you will. They were perceived to be unclean because they couldn't observe all of the ceremonial hand washings that Jews had to perform in that day. So essentially, these guys were outcasts. Yet these are the people—shepherds keeping watch over their flocks by night—to whom God chose to announce the birth of His Son.

Shepherds were nobodies, and yet God chose to honor them in this way. This gives hope to ordinary people like us. When you think about it, however, this was our Lord's mode of operation throughout His ministry. He always has appealed to the outcast, the ordinary, the common people. He made a special effort to reach out to Zacchaeus, the despised tax collector, to the woman caught in adultery, to people with leprosy, and to disabled people. What's more, He made time for little children, saying, "Let the children come to me. Don't stop them! For the Kingdom of Heaven belongs to those who are like these children" (Matthew 19:14, NLT).

Dr. Luke gives us the specifics of the announcement to the shepherds:

> Now there were in the same country shepherds living out in the fields, keeping watch over their flock by night. And behold, an angel of the Lord stood before them, and the glory of the Lord shone around them, and they were greatly afraid. Then the angel said to them, "Do not be afraid, for behold, I bring you good tidings of great joy which will be to all people. For there is born to you this day in the city of David a Savior, who is Christ the Lord. And this will be the sign to you: You will find a Babe wrapped in swaddling cloths, lying in a manger."
>
> And suddenly there was with the angel a multitude of the heavenly host praising God and saying:
>
> "Glory to God in the highest,
> And on earth peace, goodwill toward men!"
> (Luke 2:8–14)

The message that burst from the heavens that night has three wonderful characteristics.

It is personal. The angel said, "I bring you good tidings."

It is positive. "I bring you *good* tidings of *great* joy."

It is universal. The angel said the good news and great joy are for "all people."

As I've said earlier, the Christmas season can be a very difficult time for people, when emotions run high and our problems seem to be amplified. Maybe you have lost your job and are not able to buy the gifts you would like to buy this year. Maybe you're having difficulty with your marriage or one of your children. Maybe someone you loved and treasured has recently passed away. There's an empty chair at the dining room table, and it's difficult to think of Christmastime without him or her. Maybe a bunch of strange relatives have shown up on your doorstep, and you can't get rid of them.

"GOOD TIDINGS OF GREAT JOY"

Where, then, are these "good tidings of great joy" the angel spoke about? The words almost seem like mockery to us sometimes. But what are those good tidings? What is this great news?

Is it "Shop 'til you drop"?

Is it "Let it snow, let it snow"?

No, this message is a call to worship. The King has come! Immanuel has come to us! We are not alone, and we never will be alone again. Why?

We have a Savior.

According to the angels, we have a Savior. Heaven's message that night was, "For there is born to you this day in the city of David *a Savior.*" He came to save us from the power and penalty of sin. Whatever you may be going through in your life, whatever you are facing, you have a Savior. That always will be the very best of news! He has put your sin as far away from you as the east is from the west. He has buried your offenses and shame in the deepest canyons of the ocean. Because of the salvation He has brought us, the moment after we take our last breath on Earth, we go straight to Heaven.

When the skies opened before the shepherds that night and the glory came rushing in like water through a broken levee, it was as though a portal had been opened into Heaven.

Sometimes we think of Heaven as millions of miles away, beyond the most distant galaxy. Personally, I think it is much closer than that. I think we are separated from Heaven by the thinnest of veils. When the veil was pulled back on that first Christmas night, the shepherds saw directly into the supernatural world and the glory of Heaven.

We have a Savior! When we are missing someone who has departed this life for Heaven, we think about him or her during the fun times at Christmas. We look at all the beautiful bright lights and the wrapped presents under the tree and think, *If only he could be here* or *If only she could see this.* But we have to remember that we are saying this about loved ones who are looking at real angels, not little plastic angels on a tree. They are looking at the glory of God Himself, not a string of colored LED lights on the mantle. They may not be opening a present, but they are in God's presence! And we have the sure hope of being reunited with them because we have a Savior.

We have a Christ.

The angel said, "For there is born to you this day in the city of David a Savior, *who is Christ* the Lord."

The word *Christ* means "anointed one," another term for Messiah. Jesus was the fulfillment of God's promise to send His Son as the Messiah—a promise that dated all the way back to the Garden of Eden. This is a simple but profound reminder that God keeps His promises. He promised a Messiah, and a Messiah came, just as the prophets of old had predicted.

In the aftermath of our son Christopher's going to be with the Lord, Warren Wiersbe wrote me a beautiful letter. Among other things, he said to me, "Greg, we live on promises, not explanations." I liked that because some things just can't be explained. We can ask, "Why? Why? Why?" again and again. Why would God allow this?

Why would He let this happen? But He may never give us those answers on this side of Heaven.

Instead of all the explanations we might crave, God gives us promises. Jesus promised He would never leave us or forsake us. He promised us that He is preparing a place for us in His Father's house. He promised that all things would work together for good to those who love Him and are the called according to His purpose.

We have a Lord.

The angel spoke of "a Savior who is Christ *the Lord.*"

What does that mean to us? It means that we have a sovereign God who is in control of our lives. As David wrote in Psalm 31:14–15, "But I trust in you, LORD; I say, 'You are my God.' My times are in your hands" (NIV).

It is God who decides the day of your birth and God who decides the day of your death. He doesn't give you a vote on either! Sometimes we will hear of someone who lived to be ninety, and we will say, "They lived a nice long life." Then someone else lives to be nineteen years old or nine years old—or nine months or nine minutes—and we say, "That isn't fair."

I understand those thoughts and those statements. But in the end, God is in control. He is in control of my life. He is Lord. Because of this, I am indestructible until God is done with me. But when that day comes, He will call for me, and I will go—and that's how it will be for you as well. If you are a Christian, the angels will come to escort you right into the presence of the Lord.

In the meantime, I have this practical word of advice for you. Don't take your loved ones—your family and close friends—for granted. You have no guarantee they will be here next Christmas. Savor the moments with them, take lots of pictures, and together, remember the most important truths in all of life.

We have a Savior.

We have a Christ.

We have a Lord.

And we have His unspeakably wonderful promise that one day soon, we will be reunited with Him and with our loved ones who have gone on into His presence ahead of us.

13

THE TRUE GIFT OF CHRISTMAS

heard about a postal worker who was sorting through the mail and came across an unstamped, handwritten envelope addressed to God. His curiosity was piqued. Opening the envelope, he found the shaky handwriting of an elderly woman writing to God. Explaining that her life savings of $200 had been stolen, she told God that if He didn't answer her prayer to provide some money, she would have a very difficult Christmas with not very much to eat.

Moved by what he had read, the postal worker approached several of his colleagues and said, "Do you want to help this lady out?"

They were all similarly touched by the woman's plight, took up a collection, and raised $180. After putting the money into an unsigned envelope with no stamp, they gave it to a mail carrier to deliver it directly to her front door.

Obviously, this woman had a merrier Christmas than she might have. About a week later, however, they got another letter addressed to God, with the same handwriting on the front. It was clearly from this same elderly woman. Opening it up, they read,

Dear God,

Thank You for the $180 You sent for Christmas, which would have been so bleak otherwise.

PS: It was about $20 short, but it probably was one of those thieving workers at the post office!

Talk about not being appreciated!

You may have experienced a time when someone really didn't value the gift you gave him or her. It might even have been something costly, and obtaining it may have taken quite a bit of effort, but the person you gave it to didn't seem to understand the gift or appreciate it. Maybe their response made you wish you had left the price tag on it. You may have wanted to say, "That actually cost me a lot! A smile or a thank you would have been nice."

Then again, we all can probably look back on Christmases where we wished for something with all our hearts but didn't receive it.

I remember the year when I asked my mom for a bicycle—but not just *any* bicycle. I had something very specific and very wonderful in mind. In those days, the coolest bike of all was the Schwinn Sting-Ray. It had those little handlebars, a long banana seat, a small front tire, and a larger rear tire. The one I wanted actually had a stick shift on it. It was *very* cool and would have made me the envy of the neighborhood.

That was what I had asked for, and it was *all* I had asked for. I just knew that I was going to get it because I had dropped a million hints about it.

Then on Christmas Eve, after I'd gone to bed, I heard some noise in the living room. As I lay in my bed and listened, it sounded for all the world like something being removed from a box and assembled . . . my bicycle? But how could that be? The Sting-Ray came preassembled and didn't need to be put together. What were they doing? What in the world were they building?

I found out the next morning when I got up. My mother and her husband at the time bought a bicycle in a box at some drugstore, put it together, and stuck it under the tree. It wasn't a Sting-Ray. It wasn't even a Schwinn. Worse still, it had *red* tires in an era when all respectable bicycle tires were black. Riding a bike around the neighborhood with red tires would have been a huge humiliation.

What was I going to do? Digging around in the garage, I found a can of black spray paint and painted those offending tires. But then, after I rode around for fifteen minutes or so, most of the paint came off, leaving me with speckled red tires. Then the sun bleached them out, and I had speckled pink tires!

But for every disaster like the one I just described, we could probably also name times when we either received the very gift we wanted or—better still—received a gift we secretly longed for but never expected.

Maybe you've known someone in your life who always seemed to give great gifts. When you encounter someone like that, it becomes very obvious that this is a person who gives careful thought and consideration to what they give. They don't just buy the first or second thing they see to get it over with and check your name off the list.

God is the best gift giver of all.

The apostle Paul wrote,

> For the wages of sin is death, but the gift of God is eternal life in Christ Jesus our Lord. (Romans 6:23, NIV)

GIFTS AND VALUE

The greatest of all, the true gift of Christmas, is the gift of eternal life.

Why did God send His Son to Earth? Why did Jesus walk among us as a man? Why did He face rejection, scorn, mockery, spitting, torture, and a slow death on a Roman cross? It was so that God could give to you this gift, this too-wonderful-for-words present with your name attached to it.

Some of the gifts you will open at Christmas will give you some initial excitement but will quickly become dated. Everyone knows that I like new gadgets, but a new outfit or an article of clothing might be closer to your heart. Yet most everything we receive will soon become dated. The electronic gizmo will soon become old technology and archaic. The new clothes will soon move from the front of the closet to the back of the closet to a cardboard box at Goodwill.

There are other gifts you may receive that seem to grow in value over the years. Maybe you didn't realize how valuable that present really was when you first opened it. It might have been a family heirloom, like your grandfather's watch that you remember him wearing when you were a child. Or maybe it was a special drawing from one of your little ones when they were very young. Maybe you had practical grandparents who, instead of buying you toys, put money into a savings account for you every year. You might have resented it at the time, but now that the money has grown with interest, it means a lot more to you than a bunch of quickly discarded toys.

Even so, you have to be careful about getting rid of some of those classic toys. An original Darth Vader figure from the 1970s now sells for around $6,000. An original Barbie doll in its packaging is worth anywhere from $8,000 to $12,000. But alas, most of us didn't save or collect such toys; we got rid of them a couple of moves ago, and they're long gone.

God's gift, however, the gift of eternal life, only grows in value as you begin to understand what it's really all about. Just for a moment, let's consider some of the benefits of this gift.

You may have imagined that this is a benefit that only kicks in after you die. But that isn't true. This is an incredibly valuable gift that you can enjoy right now. One of the aspects of this gift of eternal life, this gift of salvation, is something called *justification*. In Romans 5:1–2 we read, "Therefore, since we have been justified through faith, we have peace with God through our Lord Jesus Christ, through whom we have gained access by faith into this grace in which we now stand" (NIV).

What we are being told here is that the very reason we can approach God, have access to God, and even be heard by God when we pray is because of this gift He has given to us.

JUSTIFICATION: A TWO-FOLD MEANING

1. What God has taken away

Justification is a unique biblical word with a two-fold meaning. First of all, it speaks of *what God has taken away.*

What has God taken away? My sin! The moment I put my faith in Jesus Christ, my sin is instantly forgiven. That might be easy for me to write or effortless for you to read, but that thought in itself is incredible! Think for a moment of all the things you have done in your life that, to this day, you regret. Those acts, those thoughts, those words you spoke, those times when you hurt someone else or hurt yourself so deeply—if you turn from those sins and call them what they are, God can forgive you because of the death of His Son on the cross. And not only will He forgive those sins, but the Bible actually says that He will *forget* those sins. Micah 7:19 tells us that He will "cast all our sins into the depths of the sea."

I love that picture!

I've done some scuba diving, and a number of years ago, I was diving over in Maui. A group of us were together in the crystal-clear waters. It was like being in another world with all the sea life and fish swimming around us. I could see the bottom about thirty feet below.

And then all of a sudden, the bottom of the ocean disappeared. With a start, I realized that we had come to the end of a shelf, and I was now over some great depth in the ocean. It was dark below me, and I couldn't see the bottom. The water seemed to go on and on forever. I wasn't any deeper in the water at that moment, but the vast depths below me made me feel very insecure. I imagined some big sea creature swimming up out of the darkness and swallowing me in a single gulp. Quickly turning around, I headed back for the security of the thirty-foot-deep shelf I had just left behind.

I've thought of that experience when I read in Micah that God has taken my sins and buried them in the depths of the ocean. That's a long, long, long way down there. As Corrie ten Boom used to say, "God casts [our sins] into the deepest ocean, gone forever. . . . I believe God then places a sign out there that says No Fishing Allowed." [1]

That's justification! He has forgiven me and chooses to forget my sins.

I have a little key on my computer keyboard with the word *delete* on it. Sometimes I write a sentence that doesn't make sense to me, and I want to get rid of it. So I highlight it and then push *delete*. It's gone! But where does it go? Does the deleted text get sent into outer space or some unseen dimension?

Frankly, I don't know, and I don't care. I just know it's gone.

In the same way, God highlights our sins, hits the delete key, and they are gone forever.

2. What God has put in place of our sins

If that is all there was to this gift of justification, it would be incredible enough. But as they say in the commercials, "But wait, there's more!" In fact, there is a very great deal more. In addition to speaking of what God has taken away, justification also speaks of what God has *put in place* of my sin. My sin is gone, and in its place is . . . the very righteousness of God Himself. The word *justified* means "to put into one's account." When God justifies a person, when a man or woman believes in Jesus, He supernaturally deposits the righteousness of Christ into his or her account.

In Acts 13:38–39 Paul declared, "Brothers! Listen! In this man Jesus there is forgiveness for your sins! Everyone who trusts in him is freed from all guilt and declared righteous—something the Jewish law could never do" (TLB). And again in 2 Corinthians 5:21 Paul said, "For He made Him who knew no sin to be sin for us, that we might become the righteousness of God in Him."

Chuck Swindoll puts it like this: "Justification is the sovereign act of God whereby He declares righteous the believing sinner while we are still in a sinning state."[2]

This is more than amazing; it's almost incomprehensible. This isn't just a huge gift; it is a God-sized gift!

Think of it like this. Imagine that you have run up a debt of $10 million. Because of your foolish excesses, you are charged with a crime and face a very long prison sentence. At your trial, someone unexpectedly shows up and says to the judge, "I am prepared to pay this person's full debt, including all interest, penalties, and fees."

As it turns out, the person is Bill Gates.

The judge pronounces you cleared of all obligations and says that you are free to go.

Turning to Bill Gates, you can hardly express your amazement and gratitude. "Oh thank you, Mr. Gates. I don't even know you, and yet you have done all this for me. I can't thank you enough! You've given me my life back."

"That's okay," he replies. "And by the way, on your way home, stop by your bank and check your balance. See what you have in your account. Good-bye."

So you do just what your benefactor has suggested that you do. On your way home, you stop at an ATM and punch in your code. You know that you used to have a balance of $2. But now you have a balance of $100 million!

That little story might seem like a stretch, but in reality, it doesn't begin to illustrate what God has done for you. First He forgave all of your sins. And then, as if that weren't enough, He deposited the righteousness of Jesus Christ, the sinless Son of God, into your account.

But wait! There's more!

ADOPTED INTO HIS FAMILY

God has not only forgiven all my sins, casting them into the deepest sea, and He has not only deposited the righteousness of His perfect Son into my account, but *He also has adopted me into His family.* Here is what the Scriptures say in Galatians 4:4–6: "But when the set time had fully come, God sent his Son, born of a woman, born under the law, to redeem those under the law, that we might receive adoption to sonship. Because you are his sons, God sent the Spirit of his Son into our hearts, the Spirit who calls out, 'Abba, Father' " (NIV).

Those three verses sum it all up, giving us the big picture of Christmas. At the appointed moment in time, the mighty angel Gabriel came to Mary and told her she would conceive supernaturally in her womb and bear a Son, whose name would be Jesus. It all took place just as the angel had said, and she gave birth to Him in the little town of Bethlehem.

He came "to redeem those under the law." That law—the commandments of God—tells us that we have all sinned and fallen short of His righteous standard. That word *redeem* means "to buy out of the slave market."

Picture yourself there. You are a slave, with a chain on your wrist and a chain shackled to your ankle. You are on the market, and people are waiting to bid on you. As you stand on the block in utter defeat and humiliation, someone speaks from near the back of the crowd and buys you at full price. Your eyes look up to see who your new owner is, and you find out that it is Jesus Himself. He says, "Look, I have set you free. You are free from the sin that has hounded you for years. You are free from that addiction. But come with Me now because there is somewhere I want to take you."

"Where is that, Lord?"

"We're going to the courthouse because I am about to adopt you as My own child and make you a part of My very own family. You are no longer a slave. You are a child of the King."

That is when you cry out, "Abba, Father!"

It's the Hebrew equivalent of saying Daddy or Papa and speaks of intimacy with God. Through our adoption as sons and daughters, God is saying to us, "Don't just stand in awe of Me. Come close to Me." As difficult as it may be for us to wrap our minds around this truth, God truly does want a personal relationship with us.

But wait! There's more!

THE LIFE TO COME

What God has given us would make life incomparably worthwhile, even if there were no afterlife. Just to know as I walk the earth that my sins are washed away, that I have the righteousness of Jesus Himself credited to my account, and that I have a relationship with Him where I can approach Him at any time—that would be enough! But there is more. And someday you and I will see with our own eyes just how *much* more.

We still have Heaven before us, after we die or when He comes for us in the clouds. Jesus said in John 17:24, "Father, I want those you have given me to be with me where I am, and to see my glory, the glory you have given me because you loved me before the creation of the world" (NIV).

Jesus is saying, "I can hardly wait to show you Heaven. I can hardly wait for you to see Me—in My splendor . . . in My glory."

When I find something that I really like, I want to share it with a friend. That's why I love to lead tours of the Holy Land. I love to take people there who are seeing it all for the first time. For those of us who love God and His Word, it's sort of like the adult version of taking a kid to Disneyland. When an adult Christian sees Jerusalem for the first time, it's a very special moment—one of the great moments of a lifetime. And I love to share those things with people I care about.

Jesus says, "I want to share My glory with you. I want you to experience it." In John 14:2 He said, "My Father's house has many rooms. . . . I am going there to prepare a place for you" (NIV). It's amazing to realize there was no room for Him in the inn, yet He has prepared many rooms for us.

All of these promises of the life to come will play out for you in real time as you leave this world and move on to the next one. This is the gift God has given you! That's why Paul said, "Thanks be to God for His indescribable gift!" (2 Corinthians 9:15). Or, as the New Living Translation puts it, "Thank God for this gift too wonderful for words!"

RED

I read a story in the newspaper recently about a terrible high school shooting where an angry student had a gun and was looking for a particular teacher he wanted to kill. The teacher got off campus quickly, but a girl was shot and killed. We have seen far too many of these school shootings, and when the students get word there's a shooter in the building, they hide themselves.

In this last shooting, a boy named Matt was hiding with some classmates and a teacher. He thought he probably was looking at his last moments on Earth. As he waited for the shooter to come, he pulled a pen and a scrap of paper out of his pocket and wrote what he thought might be his final message to his family: "Family, I love you so much. I am HERE now." Then he drew a picture of a cross, implying that he was in Heaven. Thankfully, Matt was not shot and got out safely.

But here's my thought: when you are crouching in a classroom with an armed person looking for you . . . or you are on a battlefield in a firefight . . . or you are in the critical care unit of a hospital with time ticking down on your life, this gift of eternal life in Heaven becomes incredibly, unspeakably, indescribably valuable and precious. You may think that you value it now. But on *that* day, it will be the most valuable thing you have ever possessed—not your car, not your house, not your 401k, not the gold you have stashed away.

Those things will mean nothing. They will have zero value to you. It will be the gift of eternal life that will give you hope.

On her deathbed, Queen Elizabeth I said, "All my possessions for a moment of time."[3] But no person could grant the request of that sovereign ruler.

The gift of eternal life is one that you receive now and open later. In our minds we tend to say, "Yes, later—*much* later."

But that might not be the case. Life on this side of eternity is very uncertain. That's why you want to make sure that you possess this gift and carry it in your heart and soul.

When I travel overseas, the first thing I make certain of is my passport. I want to know where it is at all times. I want to keep it secure but have it available in a moment's notice when I need it.

So it is with the gift of eternal life. We want to be sure of it. We want to know that we have it when we find ourselves—perhaps suddenly and unexpectedly—stepping out of time and into eternity.

PART THREE

CHRISTMAS, FUTURE

14

CHRISTMAS IN THE BOOK OF REVELATION

Sometimes we might think we've heard it all when it comes to Christmas.

We've read the accounts in Matthew and Luke umpteen times, heard multiple sermons, and conclude that we have the biblical account pretty much wired.

But there is more—more, perhaps, than we've ever imagined.

In Revelation 12, we see a view of Christmas from the heavenly perspective, and it isn't exactly Currier and Ives. In fact, there isn't a yule log, holly berry, snowflake, or sleigh bell to be found.

Instead of Mary and Joseph, angels and shepherds, and wise men and innkeepers, we have a different cast altogether. We have a pregnant woman being pursued by a powerful Dragon who seeks her death. As she prepares to give birth, he hovers over her, waiting to destroy her Baby.

Christmas?

Yes, but probably from an angle we've never seen before. It surely shows one thing: the original Christmas, more than two thousand years ago, was a time of great conflict in the heavens and on Earth.

To this day, Christmas is a time of conflict. The pressure in our culture to shop, buy, and pursue all-out materialism grows more insane every year. And the madness starts earlier and earlier on the calendar. Thanksgiving used to be the one day when all the malls were shut down. Not anymore. Now the retailers have decided to open their doors on Thanksgiving, starting the Christmas buying rush before Black Friday. This retailing on steroids has created and maintained a culture of chaos around the holiday season. As someone recently said, retailers have basically ruined every holiday that we have.

Did you read any accounts of last year's Black Friday sales? News reports told of crowds shattering windows, beating each other up in the aisles, and threatening one another's lives. Two people were shot outside a Walmart in Florida. One man took his girlfriend's three-year-old son to Kmart for a midnight sale. He left with a fifty-one-inch flat-screen television—but forgot the kid.

We read about Christmas traffic jams, families coming unraveled, domestic violence, and counseling offices filled with depressed, even suicidal, clients. Christmas is supposed to be a happy time, a peaceful time. But in many homes, it hasn't been that for years, if ever.

The idea of a traditional family gathering for the holidays seems to be something of the past, with so many broken homes resulting from divorce. Family gatherings can be problematic. We have to go visit Dad and his new wife, then spend time with Mom and her new live-in boyfriend. Then we have to figure out how to respond to all the stepbrothers, stepsisters, and step-in-laws.

It's awkward, uncomfortable, and seems to lend itself to all kinds of disappointments and interpersonal conflicts.

But no matter how much conflict we experience today, it can't compare to the conflict that preceded the very first Christmas when God became man.

Revelation 12 shows us that Satan didn't want there to be a Christmas at all and did everything in his power to stop the birth of Jesus on Earth. His efforts to thwart the Incarnation might have succeeded—but God intervened.

Thankfully, God always has the last word.

THE DRAGON AND WONDER WOMAN

Now a great sign appeared in heaven: a woman clothed with the sun, with the moon under her feet, and on her head a garland of twelve stars. Then being with child, she cried out in labor and in pain to give birth.

> And another sign appeared in heaven: behold, a great, fiery red dragon having seven heads and ten horns, and seven diadems on his heads. His tail drew a third of the stars of heaven and threw them to the earth. And the dragon stood before the woman who was ready to give birth, to devour her Child as soon as it was born. She bore a male Child who was to rule all nations with a rod of iron. And her Child was caught up to God and His throne. (Revelation 12:1–5)

Who is this wonder woman of Revelation 12:1?

First, let me tell you who she *isn't*. She isn't Mary, the mother of Jesus. Some in the Catholic church through the years have asserted that this is a vision of the Virgin Mary. In fact, I believe the woman in this incredible vision is actually the nation of Israel, and the Child that she bears is Jesus Christ.

Verse 1 speaks of a "garland of twelve stars." You may remember that in the dream God gave to young Joseph in Genesis 37, Israel was symbolized by a sun, a moon, and eleven stars, with Joseph being the twelfth star. That is the first instance of the imagery of twelve stars, so when it is repeated again in the book of Revelation, we make the connection that God intends us to make: both instances refer to the nation of Israel. This is called the rule of first mention.

The Messiah came from Israel, and He will one day rule over the entire Earth. In verse 5 we read that "she bore a male Child who was to rule all nations with a rod of iron." Where have we heard that expression before? Again, going back to its first mention in the Scriptures, we find those words in Psalm 2. In this messianic psalm, God the Father says to the Messiah:

> You are My Son,
> Today I have begotten You.
> Ask of Me, and I will give You
> The nations for Your inheritance,
> And the ends of the earth for Your possession.
> You shall break them with a rod of iron;
> You shall dash them to pieces like a potter's vessel.
> (verses 7–9)

There is that same picture again. The image refers to a time on Earth known as the Millennium, after the Battle of Armageddon and the second coming of Christ.

The word *millennium* means "thousand" and refers to the future thousand-year reign of Christ on Earth. At this point, as believers we will already have been raptured into Heaven and will return with Christ when He comes again in great glory. At this time, Satan will be chained and out of the way, and we will be in our glorified bodies, ruling and reigning with Jesus.

But why would Jesus need to rule Earth with "a rod of iron"?

Because during this thousand-year period, not everyone will *want* to be ruled by Christ, as difficult as that might be to believe. The survivors of the Tribulation still will be on Earth, as well as their descendants. And even though Christ's ten-century rule will be perfect in every way, there will be a short-lived rebellion at the end of the thousand years, led by the newly released Satan. After that rebellion is quickly quashed, the New Jerusalem will come down to earth out of Heaven, and we will experience the new heaven and the new earth.

Not only does Christ rule with a rod of iron during the Millennium, but we will have the privilege to rule *with* Him. In the story we refer to as the parable of the talents, the master speaks these words to a faithful servant who has wisely invested his life and resources: "Well done, good and faithful servant; you were faithful over a few things, I will make you ruler over many things. Enter into the joy of your lord" (Matthew 25:21).

Have you ever wondered what that meant? It means that as a wise steward of your life and as a faithful follower of Jesus, you will have delegated authority under the King of kings to rule and reign with Him.

THE IDENTITY OF THE DRAGON

> Behold, a great, fiery red dragon having seven heads and
> ten horns, and seven diadems on his heads. His tail drew
> a third of the stars of heaven and threw them to the earth.
> (Revelation 12:3-4)

This Dragon is none other than Satan, the fallen angel who was
once named Lucifer, son of the morning (see Isaiah 14:12). Seven
heads and ten horns sound like something out of one of those old
Godzilla movies, doesn't it?

The heads and the horns on this Dragon are symbols. The word
head comes from the word *diadem*, which also could be translated
"crown." This symbolizes power, authority, and intelligence, and Satan
possesses all of these things. Our adversary has vast intelligence
and has had thousands of years to perfect his craft of attacking
men and women and wreaking chaos, pain, sorrow, and havoc
on Earth. In 2 Corinthians 4:3-4 we read,

> If the Good News we preach is hidden to anyone, it is hid-
> den from the one who is on the road to eternal death.
> Satan, who is the god of this evil world, has made him
> blind, unable to see the glorious light of the Gospel that is

shining upon him or to understand the amazing message we preach about the glory of Christ, who is God. (TLB)

Satan, whom Paul labels as "the god of this world," is so clever that he has fooled many people into thinking he doesn't even exist—while in reality, he controls their very lives.

The ten horns spoken of in this passage refer to ten confederated nations that will be working with Antichrist at this time. Later we will read that it is the Dragon who gives Antichrist his authority. In other words, Satan energizes this charismatic coming world leader who will have ten nations working together with him. (More about this later.)

In Revelation 12:4 we read that this Dragon "drew a third of the stars of heaven and threw them to the earth." This refers to the circumstances of Satan's fall, when he took one-third of the angels of Heaven with him. These fallen angels, or demons, now do his dirty work in our world. They are Satan's storm troopers, if you will.

Notice the fierce anger and aggression of this Dragon in verse 4: "The dragon stood before the woman who was ready to give birth, to devour her Child as soon as it was born."

Here are two things you need to bear in mind about Satan: (1) he is anti-Semitic, and (2) he is anti-Christ. He hates Israel, and he hates Jesus Christ and all who belong to Him. He has nurtured a special hatred for the Jewish people from the days of Pharaoh to Haman to Hitler to Stalin to Iran to Hamas.

He would devour Israel in a moment—if he could. So far he hasn't been able to. But he will keep trying.

SATAN HATES CHRISTMAS

These graphic images in Revelation 12 give us the big picture of what Christmas is really all about—and why Satan hates it with everything in him. I believe we are witnessing this hatred in our own culture as we see increasingly bold atheistic groups that are hell-bent on killing Christmas in the Western world. They don't want manger scenes on public property. They don't want Christmas carols in public schools. In some cities, officials even have banned innocuous Christmas trees.

I don't even know if these anti-Christmas activists fully understand what they are doing. In fact, I very much doubt they do. I am reminded of the Lord's statement from the cross, when He prayed for those who had crucified Him, saying, "Father, forgive them, for they do not know what they do" (Luke 23:34).

The banning of manger scenes in public places, the banning of Christmas carols from public schools and public events, and all hostility toward Jesus Christ is directly linked to the Dragon in

Revelation 12, waiting with bared fangs to devour the Child that is about to be born.

The Devil, who hates both Jewish people and their Messiah, knows exactly what he is doing. It is a cosmic feud that goes all the way back to the first book of the Bible. In fact, it goes back to the very first Christmas passage—the first messianic passage—in the Bible. God speaks these words in Genesis 3:15, after Adam and Eve sinned against Him and ate of the forbidden fruit: "I will put enmity between you and the woman, between your seed and her Seed; He shall bruise your head, and you shall bruise His heel."

The Lord was putting Satan on notice. A Coming One would crush his head, while Satan only would manage to bruise His heel. This is speaking of Jesus, who doomed and crushed the head of Satan on the cross. But the Devil did bruise the Lord's heel. Speaking of the coming Messiah in Isaiah 53, the prophet told us, "He was wounded for our transgressions, He was bruised for our iniquities; the chastisement for our peace was upon Him, and by His stripes we are healed" (verse 5).

At the cross, Satan was crushed and Jesus was bruised. By the way, that is precisely how to kill a snake. You crush his head. Don't ever pick up a snake by the tail, because it can rear around and bite you. No, you have to smash your heel down on its head, which is exactly what Christ did.

From this announcement in Genesis, then, Satan knew there would be a Coming One from the woman's seed who would crush his head. In time, he would understand that this future Savior would come from the Jewish race.

In Exodus, Satan worked through Pharaoh, seeking to kill all the Jewish boys at birth. In the book of Judges, we can see Satan using Israel's neighbors as they sought to destroy the nation. In 1 Samuel, we see Saul trying to murder David, thus stopping the messianic line. In Esther, we have the plot of the anti-Semitic Haman to wipe out Jews all over the world.

All of these murderous plots failed, but Satan wasn't done yet, not by a long shot. Having failed to wipe out the people of God in the messianic line, he attempted to murder the Messiah Himself before He could do His saving work. Remember when those mysterious wise men blew into town, having seen a star in the East? These Magi wanted to locate, honor, and worship the newborn King of the Jews. That was the last thing you wanted to say to a paranoid powder-keg tyrant like King Herod. The fact of the matter is that Caesar had given *him* the title "king of the Jews."

This announcement from the wise men seemed like a direct threat to his throne. After checking the matter out with his scholars, he determined this royal baby would be born in Bethlehem. So what did Herod do? He sent his soldiers to Bethlehem to put to death all the baby boys under the age of two, in a nightmare attempt to put an end to this newborn Messiah.

But God had warned Joseph in a dream to flee to Egypt, frustrating Herod's (and Satan's) murderous plan.

Christ was born and grew into manhood. But the attacks continued. At the very outset of His ministry, Satan tempted Him in the wilderness. At one point the Devil showed Jesus all the kingdoms of the world in a moment of time. The Evil One said to Jesus, "All these things I will give You if You will fall down and worship me" (Matthew 4:9).

Jesus never challenged or refuted Satan's statement. If it had been a lie, Jesus would have confronted that lie. But what Satan said in that moment was technically true. At this time, Satan is "the god of this world" and has control of the kingdoms of the world. The Devil was saying to Jesus, in effect, "Look, Jesus, we both know why You are here. You are here to purchase back that which was lost in the Garden of Eden. But there's no need to battle for it. I will give You that title deed to the world on a silver platter. There doesn't have to be a cross, or suffering, or bearing the sins of the world. I'll give all that to You in this moment if You only will give me the satisfaction of bowing down and worshiping me."

Of course Jesus resisted and refuted Satan, saying, "Away with you, Satan! For it is written, 'You shall worship the LORD your God, and Him only you shall serve' " (Matthew 4:10).

Satan wanted to divert Jesus from His course. But Jesus refused to be diverted.

The attacks continued after Jesus began His ministry. They even tried to put Him to death in His hometown of Nazareth. A mob actually took Christ to the edge of a cliff and were preparing to push Him off, but the Bible tells us in Luke 4 that He calmly passed through their midst and went on His way.

Why was He able to walk away from a murderous mob that were hell-bent on killing Him? Because it wasn't His time. His hour had not yet come.

As I mentioned earlier in this book, you, as a Christian, are indestructible until God is done with you. But when your hour comes, when your date with destiny arrives, when your moment to enter eternity is here, there is nothing you can do to change it. That is why you want to live your life well and for the glory of God in the interim.

And then His hour finally came. What was that hour?

It was the hour where He would suffer and die for the sins of the world. As Jesus told His captors in the Garden of Gethsemane, "Every day I was with you in the temple courts, and you did not lay a hand on me. But this is your hour—when darkness reigns" (Luke 22:53, NIV).

In a way, it could look as though the Devil had prevailed. Jesus was betrayed by Judas Iscariot, tried by a kangaroo court, sentenced to death by Pilate, crucified on a cross, and then buried in a borrowed tomb.

But then God raised Him from the dead, opening the door for our eternal salvation.

The whole purpose of Christmas was that Jesus was born on Earth so that He might live a perfect life and one day die for our sins. The birth of Jesus happened to make possible the death of Jesus. That is why, to this day, Satan, the Dragon, wants to kill the real meaning of Christmas. Frankly, the Devil doesn't care if you shop till you drop, decorate your house with a million lightbulbs, or get drunk at the office party. But if you take the time to contemplate what Christmas is all about and worship the newborn King, he will be angry. If he can't stop Christmas altogether, he will settle for hiding its meaning.

TOO BEAUTIFUL?

I began this book by suggesting that the problem with our Christmas celebrations is that we have made them all too beautiful. We love all the images of sleighs and snow, delight in the fragrance of Christmas candles and freshly baked goodies, take pleasure in all the brightly wrapped packages under the tree, and lose ourselves in the lovely music of the holiday. The celebration can be beautiful.

But the story itself is wrapped in tragedy: a little baby was born to spill His blood and die on a cross in the prime of a perfect life. That is why red is the color of Christmas. It isn't because Santa wears red, because holly berries are red, or because we like red wrapping paper. Christmas is red because that's the color of the blood of Jesus that was shed from the cross. He was born to die so that we might live.

Sometimes in our attempts to beautify and sanitize Christmas, we might miss the essential message.

That's why this vision in the book of Revelation, portraying the heavenly perspective of Christmas, is so startling. Instead of the soft, fragrant, gentle elements we're used to in our celebrations, we see a pregnant woman crying out in pain, a fearsome, fiery red Dragon, and a Child snatched from the jaws of destruction.

Yes, the Dragon's plan to stop Christmas—or, more specifically, the birth of Jesus Christ—was thwarted, and his whole plan backfired (for him) in the worst way possible. But he still hates every reminder of the Child who came to die. Why? Because that Child became a Man who sealed his doom.

THE BATTLE GOES ON

What did God say when He announced in Genesis 3:15 that the Messiah was coming? He said to the Devil, "I will put enmity between you and the woman, and between your seed and her

Seed; He shall bruise your head, and you shall bruise His heel."

In other words, this isn't just a battle between God and Satan; it is between Satan's *seed* and God's *seed*.

Who is God's seed? That is us, all the true followers of Jesus around the world. By contrast, Satan's seed are those who follow the Devil. There is no middle ground, and there are no neutral countries in this ceaseless warfare. In reality, you are either following God right now, or you are following Satan.

Someone might say, "I don't agree. I don't even *believe* in God or Satan."

That really changes nothing. If you don't believe and follow God's Son, the Bible says that you have been blinded by the god of this world who is controlling your life.

This is the battle between God's seed and Satan's seed. Like it or not, as a follower of Jesus you will face hostility because of that fact. Jesus said very clearly, "If the world hates you, you know that it hated Me before it hated you. If you were of the world, the world would love its own. Yet because you are not of the world, but I chose you out of the world, therefore the world hates you" (John 15:18–19).

"That is not very nice," someone may say. "I don't like all this talk about hate."

I don't either, but that is the reality of the world we live in, a world wrapped in an ancient warfare. The truth is that if you dare to speak up for Jesus Christ, publically acknowledging that you love Him and belong to Him, then you will be treated differently. You will begin to be treated as He was treated.

Our choice, then, as believers is to either fight in the spiritual battle or be overcome and overtaken by the Enemy. We can choose victory or defeat, winning or losing, advancing or retreating.

Simply put, Satan doesn't want you to follow Christ, and he will do all in his power to keep you from doing that.

Remember the Dragon in Revelation 12! He wanted to devour the Son being born two thousand years ago, and to this day he wants to devour all who belong to Him. The conflict between God's seed and Satan's seed will rage until the very end. In the end, those who belong to Jesus Christ will overcome.

That's the real story of Christmas.

15

BE READY FOR HIS COMING

For all the effort our secular world puts into stamping out the memory and traditions of Christmas, you can still see it coming.

You've probably seen the telltale signs in your town and in your neighborhood. The lights are going up on houses. These days, you see more of those giant inflatable Frosty the Snowmen and Rudolph the Red-Nosed Reindeers. Now and then, and not as often as in days gone by, you will see a manger scene in someone's yard.

You see Christmas trees on the tops of cars and traffic backing up around the malls. And you can throw your back out by lifting your morning newspaper, stuffed as it is with a thousand slick advertising pieces. And then of course there are the nonstop commercials promoting every article or service under the sun as a Christmas gift.

I was watching a cartoon on TV with my granddaughter Stella the other day, and after one of the toy commercials she said, "Papa, can you get that for me? Will you get that for me?"

"I don't know, Stella," I said. "I don't think I like that last toy. Let me find one that's really cool. If I see a cool toy, maybe I'll get it."

Then the next toy ad came on, and she said, "Papa, was that cool enough?"

Ah, the pressure is on! Everyone on all sides is pushing us to get out there and spend our money in order to "celebrate" this season. I don't think it's possible to miss the fact that Christmas is here.

As I've said in this book, however, many people did miss that first Christmas when Jesus was born in Bethlehem. In fact, most people in the world missed it.

Of course there weren't the telltale signs we have today. There were no reindeer on anyone's front lawn back then and no Christmas carols to hear quite yet. There were no brightly colored lights hanging from the little huts that people would have been living in and no sales at the downtown market. There were no colorfully wrapped presents and so forth. And most likely, children didn't find it hard at all to sleep that night because it was a night like any other—or so it seemed.

But it isn't as though the people of Israel didn't have signs and signals that something special was in the air. Godly men and women must have had the sense that the coming of the Messiah was near.

We have already spoken of godly Simeon who had God's personal word on it:

And behold, there was a man in Jerusalem whose name

was Simeon, and this man was just and devout, waiting for the Consolation of Israel, and the Holy Spirit was upon him. And it had been revealed to him by the Holy Spirit that he would not see death before he had seen the Lord's Christ. (Luke 2:25–26)

When he saw the baby Jesus in the temple with Mary and Joseph, the Holy Spirit whispered to him, "This is the One!"

About the same time, they were approached by an elderly saint named Anna, who also recognized the infant Jesus as the Messiah, and "she gave thanks to the Lord, and spoke of Him to all those who looked for redemption in Jerusalem" (Luke 2:38).

Right after the disciple Philip had met Jesus, he hurried off to tell Nathanael about it, saying, "We have found the very person Moses and the prophets wrote about! His name is Jesus, the son of Joseph from Nazareth" (John 1:45, NLT).

The woman at the well in Sychar, even though she was a Samaritan, also was looking for the Messiah. Before she recognized Jesus for who He was, she said, "I know that Messiah is coming. . . . When He comes, He will tell us all things" (John 4:25).

There's no doubt about it: even after four hundred years of silence, there were those in Israel who had stayed on their tiptoes, watching and waiting for the appearance of the Messiah.

The Hebrew prophets had clearly foretold the fact that a Savior was coming, that He would indeed be the Messiah, that He would be born of a virgin, that He would be a direct descendent of David's, and that He would be born in the tiny village of Bethlehem.

For the most part, however, people missed those signs.

Why?

It's because they really weren't paying attention.

Life was difficult under Roman occupation, and most people just plodded along, trying to make a living and attempting to stay out of trouble with the authorities. The Jewish leaders and scholars, though they had their heads filled with biblical content, had become completely absorbed in the minutiae of all the extra laws, regulations, and traditions that had been added to the Law over the generations. In fact, they were so distracted that they didn't recognize the Messiah when He was standing right in front of them.

Things were spiritually dark for Israel in those days. No one had seen an angel or heard from a prophet or witnessed a miracle in living memory. Demons were abroad in the land, possessing men and women in frightening ways and inflicting diseases.

Even so, things were ripe for the arrival of the Messiah—and the godly people in the land sensed it and watched for it.

Sadly, however, many people in Israel were spiritually asleep when God visited them that first Christmas. It's pretty much the same as we look at our own culture today. Yes, we celebrate Christmas, but it is so easy to forget about Christ.

You and I, however, can make sure we are ready when He returns to Earth as He has promised. Jesus Christ, born in the manger in Bethlehem, crucified on the cross of Calvary, and risen from the dead, is coming back again.

That may not be a popular topic of discussion, but it doesn't make it any less true. Some people don't want to talk about the Rapture or the Second Coming and shrug it off as a fad or as something of little importance. That's just what the apostle Peter said people would do:

> I want to remind you that in the last days there will come scoffers who will do every wrong they can think of and laugh at the truth. This will be their line of argument: "So Jesus promised to come back, did he? Then where is he? He'll never come! Why, as far back as anyone can remember, everything has remained exactly as it was since the first day of creation." (2 Peter 3:3–4, TLB)

Those who have been watching and waiting, however, know that He will come soon—and we don't want to miss that! He came right on schedule the first time, and He will come right on schedule the second time. The book of Galatians tells us, "But when the set time had fully come, God sent his Son, born of a woman" (4:4, NIV).

Jesus was born in Bethlehem when the time was just right. He wasn't early, and He wasn't late. And it will be the same way when He comes back again. He will come when the time is just right, the time set by His Father.

For those whose eyes are open, for those who are alert and watching, the signs and signals of His soon return are everywhere. There are 260 chapters in the New Testament, and Christ's return is mentioned no less than 318 times in these chapters. It is a recurring theme in the Bible. In John 14:3, Jesus Himself said, "And if I go and prepare a place for you, I will come again and receive you to Myself; that where I am, there you may be also."

In Mark 8:38, Jesus spoke of the time He will come "in the glory of His Father with the holy angels."

As we watch things going from bad to worse in our cities, in our nation, and in our world, we may sometimes find ourselves wondering, *Lord, are You really paying attention to Planet Earth? Do You realize how bad it has gotten?*

The answer is yes. He is fully aware of everything that is happening (and an infinite number of things that you're not aware of).

Regarding the timing of His coming, Jesus said, "But of that day and hour no one knows" (Matthew 24:36). Translate that out of the original language, and He said, "But of that day and hour no one knows." Explaining it carefully, it means, "But of that day and hour no one knows."

So if you hear some teacher on the radio or a preacher on the TV say that he knows the day of the Lord's return, then go ahead and change the station. Flip the channel. He doesn't know what he's talking about, because Jesus said *no one knows*. Period.

But if we can't know the specific date, we can discern the *season* that we're in. Jesus said in Matthew 16:2–3, "You know the saying, 'Red sky at night means fair weather tomorrow; red sky in the morning means foul weather all day.' You know how to interpret the weather signs in the sky, but you don't know how to interpret the signs of the times!" (NLT).

Early this morning, it was raining outside my house. How did I know that? Well, it was like this: I walked outside, and it rained on me. By the way, bald men are always the first to know when it's raining. I will be walking down the street with my wife, and I will say, "It's raining."

She'll say, "No, it's not." But she has so much hair that she wouldn't know if it was a hurricane.

I will reply, "Yes, it *is* raining. I feel the drops on my head!"

No, we can't know the day or the hour of Christ's return, but we can learn to read the signs of the times. And those signs have been saying consistently and clearly that the time for our Lord's return is near.

You might ask, "What are those signs?"

I could write a book on that. (In fact, I have.) First of all, I would mention the regathering of the nation of Israel into their ancient homeland. That is not only a sign, it is a *supersign.* God predicted that the nation of Israel would be dispersed to the four corners of the Earth and that in the last days, they would be regathered and become a nation once again, surrounded by hostile enemies. And that is exactly what has happened with Israel today.

There is no historical precedent for such a thing happening with any other nation in the world. But against all odds, Israel reformed as a nation on May 14, 1948, after having reestablished themselves in their homeland.

The Bible tells us that not only would Israel have hostile, dangerous enemies, but there would be weapons with the capacity to destroy our planet. The book of Revelation and other Scripture passages offer vivid descriptions of catastrophic devastation. And today we have the technology at our fingertips to fulfill some of these terrifying Bible prophecies.

I read recently that the nation of Iran, a sworn enemy of Israel, now claims the ability to produce yellow-cake uranium, which means they are a step closer to producing their own nuclear weapons. What's more, that nation has threatened to use nuclear weapons against the nation they call "the little Satan," or Israel. The nation they call "the great Satan," of course, is the United States of America.

These are clear signs of the times, yet many—including people you work with, go to school with, or live next door to—look on these developments and events with complete indifference. There are people today who have a better handle on how to prepare for a Christmas celebration than how to prepare for the return of Jesus Christ.

WHAT ARE WE TO DO?

What are we to do in light of the fact that Christ is coming again? We don't have to wonder or be in the dark. Jesus tells us Himself:

> Be dressed for service and keep your lamps burning, as though you were waiting for your master to return from the wedding feast. Then you will be ready to open the door and let him in the moment he arrives and knocks. The servants who are ready and waiting for his return will be rewarded. I tell you the truth, he himself will seat them, put on an apron, and serve them as they sit and eat! He may come in the middle of the night or just before dawn. But whenever he comes, he will reward the servants who are ready.

Understand this: If a homeowner knew exactly when a burglar was coming, he would not permit his house to be broken into. You also must be ready all the time, for the Son of Man will come when least expected. (Luke 12:35–40, NLT)

When we read an account like this, it might be hard for us to grasp sometimes, because it is relating to a long-ago and far-away culture, back in biblical times. What Jesus was describing was a classic first-century Jewish wedding. Unlike our weddings today, a first-century Hebrew wedding would last *days* rather than hours. It was an extended time of celebration and fun. One of the fun elements was the fact that you didn't know when the groom was coming. The bridal party would be assembled, the bridesmaids would be prepared, and the groomsmen would be ready.

But where was the groom?

With no warning, an announcement would be made: "The groom is coming!"

If you were asleep or off doing this or that, you might miss the ceremony. It might come in the middle of the night, or it might come early in the morning at first light. You simply had to *be* ready and *stay* ready, sleeping in your wedding clothes if you had to. The groom suddenly would be in your midst, and the ceremony would begin.

Jesus was saying, "That's how it will be when I return. Be ready. Be alert. Don't be overly preoccupied with other things." The New King James Version says, "Let your waist be girded and your lamps burning" (verse 35).

What does it mean to have your waist girded? Back in those days, they wore long, flowing robes with a belt. When they wanted to cinch up their robes for easier movement, they would tuck them into their belts. These belts also would have objects attached. For instance, they would sometimes carry an extra flask of oil for their lamps. (It would be like having extra alkaline batteries for your flashlight.) Their lamps were saucerlike, filled with oil and a floating wick. When your oil got low, you would pull out your little flask and replenish your lamp.

Jesus was saying, "Keep your robe cinched up and tucked into your belt so that you can move fast when you need to." In other words, put those fresh batteries in that flashlight. Gas up your car. Have your cell phone charged to the max. Be ready to roll at a moment's notice.

And that is how we are to be in anticipation of our Lord's return.

When Christ comes, you won't have time to change anything. You won't be able to say, "Well, I need to wrap up a couple of things first."

There will be no time. It will occur in a millisecond—the twinkling of an eye, as the Scriptures say. So you just need to be ready and stay ready, because you could be walking from the kitchen into the living room and suddenly find yourself swept up into the clouds. You could be having a conversation with a friend, and suddenly you're with the Lord in the air. That is how fast the Rapture will happen, and it could take place at any moment. There is nothing left on the prophetic calendar that has to happen before Jesus returns for His church.

Jesus made an interesting statement in Luke 12:38: "And if he should come in the second watch, or come in the third watch, and find them so, blessed are those servants."

What does that mean? Back in those days, they divided the night into four watches, or shifts. The first watch was from 6:00 p.m. to 9:00 p.m. The second was from 9:00 p.m. to 12:00 a.m. The third was from 12:00 a.m. to 3:00 a.m. And the fourth watch of the night included the time just before dawn.

So Jesus was saying, in effect, "If I come later than you originally expected, be ready." It's another reminder to us that Christ will come right on time—*His* time. The apostle Peter tells us, "The Lord is not slow in keeping his promise, as some understand slowness. Instead he is patient with you, not wanting anyone to perish, but everyone to come to repentance" (2 Peter 3:9, NIV).

I believe that Jesus Christ is waiting for that last person to believe so that we can all go to Heaven. Who is that last person? Wouldn't it be nice to know? I think we might be tempted to pressure that person just a bit, don't you? We might say to him or her, "Hey, are you going to get saved or what?"

Whoever it may be, when that last person says yes to Jesus, we all will be caught up into the clouds to meet the Lord in the air.

So what are we supposed to be doing until the Lord comes back? Several things, according to Luke 12.

1. We are to be watching for Him.

"Blessed are those servants whom the master, when he comes, will find watching" (verse 37).

This doesn't mean we're to stand around like idiots, staring into the sky. To *watch* simply means to be alert and aware. For instance, when I read the newspaper or go to a news website, I'm always thinking about world news and national news in terms of the signs of the times. So I'm not just seeing another conflict in the Middle East or reading about an economic meltdown in Europe or noting that North Korea has threatened to use its nuclear weapons. I'm looking for things that might point to biblical signs and indicators that the day of the Lord's return is near.

Jesus said, "Now when these things begin to happen, look up and lift up your heads, because your redemption draws near" (Luke 21:28). The Bible also says, "He will appear a second time, not to bear sin, but to bring salvation to those who are waiting for him" (Hebrews 9:28, NIV).

So be watching.

2. We are to be ready to go.

As Christmas approaches, most of us have a to-do list. We want to get the house decorated, the shopping done, and maybe a menu planned for when company arrives. That means *before* December 24! It won't help to get ready for Christmas after Christmas is over. So here's a word to the wise, especially if you're a guy: Don't let Christmas Eve come as a revelation to you. Make sure you've thought through what you're getting for your wife or your girlfriend. You'll have a happier Christmas if you're ready!

Referring to the coming of Jesus, the Scriptures are saying to us, "Be ready to go. Have your bags packed. Have your shirt sleeves rolled up. Have your comfortable shoes on. Be ready to depart at a moment's notice."

This is the question we need to ask ourselves: Am I ready?

You don't want to be engaged in some activity that you'd be ashamed of if Jesus suddenly returned. This is an interesting question to ask yourself periodically: Is this place I'm about to go, or this thing I'm ready to do, something that I would be ashamed of or embarrassed to be involved with if Jesus were to come back?

If the answer to that question is yes, then I would suggest that you don't do it.

If you really believe that Christ could return at any moment, then it will have a practical impact on the way that you live. In 1 John 3 the apostle says, "Beloved, now we are children of God; and it has not yet been revealed what we shall be, but we know that when He is revealed, we shall be like Him, for we shall see Him as He is. And everyone who has this hope in Him purifies himself, just as He is pure" (verses 2–3).

In other words, the stronger I hold to the truth about Christ's any-moment return, the more it will impact how I live my life.

Have you ever noticed how people behave differently when a uniformed police officer enters the room? I have a few friends who are police officers, and I was meeting with one for coffee the other day. When we walked into that little coffee place together, the whole atmosphere of the room changed. People began confessing stuff to him: "I really wasn't speeding that much on my way over here." He just laughed.

Or have you noticed how the flow of traffic changes when the highway patrol merges onto the freeway? Everyone slows down, and no one wants to be the one to pass that officer. We alter our activity because we are aware of the presence of an authority figure. In the same way, knowing that Jesus could merge into our world at literally any second ought to affect the way that we live, what we do, and what we say.

3. We should not only be ready for His return, but we should anxiously await His return.

"*And you yourselves be like men who wait for their master, when he will return from the wedding, that when he comes and knocks they may open to him immediately*" (Luke 12:36).

Have you ever dreaded the arrival of someone at your house? Do you remember what that felt like and how you didn't even want to answer the door?

Then again, have you ever looked forward to someone's arrival, and before they could even knock, you opened the door? That is how we should be when we think of the return of Jesus, looking forward to that moment with anticipation and joy and not dreading it at all.

In the book of Revelation, in the second-to-last verse of the Bible, Jesus said, "Surely I am coming quickly" (22:20).

And the response of every true Christian should be, "Amen. Even so, come, Lord Jesus!" (verse 20).

Anything that would prevent us from answering in that way is out of place in our lives. Anything that would make it difficult for us to say, "Come quickly, Lord Jesus" is actually spiritual weakness and a dangerous area to us.

4. We are not only to be waiting, but we are also to be working.

"*Blessed* is *that servant whom his master will find so doing when he comes*" (Luke 12:43).

If watching is the evidence of faith, then working is the evidence of faith in action. Watching for the Lord's return will help us prepare our own lives, but working will assure that we bring others with us. We should be using the days and years of our lives to serve the Lord—and to look for every opportunity to tell people about Jesus.

This is a happy way to live. Luke 12:37 says, "Blessed are those servants whom the master, when he comes, will find watching." This verse could be translated, "*Oh how happy are those servants.*"

Watching daily for the Lord's return isn't a miserable, repressive, confining way to live; it's a happy, joyful, purposeful way to live.

So yes, Christmas is coming, and the signs are all around us.

But the fact is that it's just a holiday. Most of us will quickly forget the gifts we receive. In fact, most of us can't remember the gifts we received last year. Christmas will come and go, whether we're ready for it or not. But when it comes to Jesus Christ returning to Earth, being ready couldn't be more important. People may have missed the first Christmas, but we don't want to miss His return. He is coming for those who are watching and waiting.

So don't just be ready for Christmas this year. Be ready for Christ Himself.

CONCLUSION

"GOD WITH US"

Children's toys today have become unbelievably more complex and elaborate than the toys of previous generations.

Back in 1960, I remember asking—begging—for a Mr. Machine for Christmas. At that time, this was a toy on the very edge of technological sophistication. And I was wildly excited to discover that I actually had it waiting for me that year under the tree.

As I remember, it didn't plug in and didn't have any batteries. By winding a large metal key on Mr. Machine's back, however, he would roll forward, legs and arms moving and bell ringing, and he would open his mouth and squawk. You could rotate a little wheel behind the toy to make it run in a circle or curve instead of moving in a straight line. And that was about it.

I remember thinking that it looked so cool and futuristic, and I felt pretty happy about it until my buddy came over with his new toy.

I had never seen anything like it. It was a little battery-operated, plastic scuba diver, outfitted with dual tanks just like Lloyd Bridges on the old *Sea Hunt* TV series. When you turned it on, the legs kicked.

You could put it in your bathtub or wading pool, and it sank to the bottom with bubbles coming out the top.

It was absolutely the edgiest technology I had ever seen. And suddenly I wasn't so happy with my Mr. Machine. I wanted a plastic scuba diver too.

The funny thing is that as you get older, things really don't change much. What's that old saying? "The only difference between men and boys is the price of their toys." And that's why Christmas is such a letdown for so many people—children and otherwise—because there is such a buildup surrounding the giving and getting of presents.

Here's the basic problem: No matter what you receive, no matter how high the price tag or elaborate the technology, "things" always will disappoint you. If that's what Christmas is all about for you, then the holiday always will be a synonym for disappointment.

That's why all of the people out there who work so tirelessly to take Jesus Christ out of Christmas will receive exactly what they want: a meaningless holiday with an emphasis on material possessions and acquiring stuff.

If, however, you want to have the merriest Christmas of all, if you want to experience Christmas the way it was meant to be experienced, then you need to understand and embrace the essential message of the season, which is simply this: *Immanuel. God is with us.*

CONCLUSION

The first chapter of the gospel of Matthew lays it out for us:

So all this was done that it might be fulfilled which was spoken by the Lord through the prophet, saying: "Behold, the virgin shall be with child, and bear a Son, and they shall call His name Immanuel," which is translated, "God with us." (verses 22–23)

Did Joseph and Mary really have any concept at all about the Child who was to enter their lives? When Mary (probably no more than a young teenager, as we have said) gave birth to her Baby in that inhospitable place, wrapped Him in strips of rags, and placed Him in a manger—possibly in the back of some cave near Bethlehem—did she grasp who He was? Did she know that the Child she nursed and held in her arms was the Savior of the world? Did she have any comprehension that her little one was *God* in human form?

Most of us have heard the contemporary Christmas song "Mary, Did You Know?":

Did you know that your baby boy has walked where angels
    trod?
And when you kiss your little baby, you have kissed the
    face of God.

Did she? Did she know? Did she understand that this was Immanuel, God with us?

What a staggering thought that is, not just for Mary, but for any of us. "God with us" is the very essence of the Christian experience. All other religions basically lay out things that you must *do* to somehow reach God or make it to Heaven or achieve Nirvana or simply escape wrath. You must do this and this and this and this. And if you do it all perfectly, then maybe you will gain the approval of God or reach the outskirts of Heaven.

In contrast to all the other religions of the world, Christianity doesn't say do; it says done! Our salvation was accomplished by God Himself, for us.

How? It was because of Immanuel, God with us. God became a man and took our penalty upon Himself.

Christmas is a lonely time of year for many people. Some people dread the month of December, wishing they could skip right from Thanksgiving to New Year's Day. Maybe there are parents with an empty nest who miss the hustle and bustle of Christmases past. Maybe someone has lost a spouse to death, and memories of Christmas only seem to make the pain and desolation harder to bear. Or perhaps a marriage broke up or has been strained, and all the holiday celebrations seem empty and sad.

Is that a description of you? Is this a time of anxiety for you or a time of separation? Are you lonely and feel as though you have no one at all?

What is loneliness? It is a painful sense of being unwanted, unloved, unneeded, uncared for, and maybe even unnecessary. Studies have shown that one of the main reasons people commit suicide is because deep down inside, they are lonely.

That's why the name Immanuel is so inexpressibly powerful.

GOD . . . IS . . . WITH . . . YOU.

He didn't just say that; He *named* Himself that.

You are not alone, and that's what God would have you understand right now.

HE UNDERSTANDS YOUR SORROWS

Did it ever cross your mind that Jesus of Nazareth might have been the loneliest man who ever lived?

You say, "Greg, what are you talking about? Jesus had His disciples."

Yes, He did. But the Bible tells us that "even in his own land and among his own people, the Jews, he was not accepted. Only a few would welcome and receive him" (John 1:11–12, TLB). The Old Testament prophet, writing of Jesus' life, said of Him: "We despised him and rejected him—a man of sorrows, acquainted with bitterest grief. We turned our backs on him and looked the other way when he went by. He was despised, and we didn't care" (Isaiah 53:3, TLB).

Those disciples of His couldn't even stay awake to watch with Him in the greatest crisis of His life, and when a murderous mob descended on the Lord, they all took off to save their own skins, leaving Him to be condemned, abused, and to die.

On the cross, with His life slipping away inch by agonizing inch and bearing the weight of all the sins of all time on His shoulders, Jesus even experienced a separation from God the Father, who turned away from Him. He called out from the cross, "My God, My God, why have You forsaken Me?" (Matthew 27:46).

Jesus knows all about loneliness. He can be with you in a special way if you are feeling lonely this Christmas. His name is Immanuel, God with *you*.

Here is what Jesus has promised to every man or woman, boy or girl, who has ever put his or her faith in Him:

> I will never leave you nor forsake you. . . . And be sure of this: I am with you always, even to the end of the age. (Hebrews 13:5, NKJV; Matthew 28:20, NLT)

That is the bottom line of this book and the bottom line of life itself: Jesus, and Jesus alone, will meet your needs—not Christmas presents and not even family and friends. People, even good people who love you, will let you down in some way, shape, or form. You and I have let down people, and we've been let down by people in turn. But Jesus never will let you down. He alone is the answer to loneliness, and He will live with you, beside you, and within you.

Without question, that is one of the most remarkable teachings in all the Bible—that somehow, some way, but in literal fact, Christ Himself enters into the human heart and lives there. The Bible clearly teaches this, whether we're able to wrap our minds around it or not. In fact, our Lord said in John 14:23, "If anyone loves Me, he will keep My word; and My Father will love him, and We will come to him and make Our home with him."

Don't let this sound like a bunch of religious jargon to you. It's as real as the chair you're sitting on right now, as real as the air you're drawing into your lungs. Jesus is saying, "My Father and I want to come and set up house with you. We want to live inside of you."

No, I don't understand it very well, either. But I know this: no matter what, I am not alone in life, and I *never* will be alone in life. And neither are you—no matter what you are going through right now, no matter what difficulty or crisis or heartbreak you might be facing, no matter what impossibility looms on the path ahead of you.

God is with you, not in an abstract, theoretical way, but in fact, in truth, and in person. God said in the book of Isaiah, "When you pass through the waters, I will be with you; and through the rivers, they shall not overflow you. When you walk through the fire, you shall not be burned" (43:2).

Are you going through a river of difficulty this Christmas? Maybe you find yourself in a fire of oppression. Remember, you are not alone. God is with you.

Maybe your marriage has been badly bruised or has fallen completely apart this year. Perhaps your children have forgotten about you. But God is with you, and He has *not* forgotten about you.

Maybe you find yourself isolated in a hospital or in a convalescent home or in a prison cell. I get letters from people writing me from these places all the time. But you are not alone in that place. God is with you as well.

That is the essential message of Christmas: God is with us.

HE WANTS TO BE PART OF YOUR LIFE

Have you asked Jesus into your life?

I think Revelation 3:20 is one of my favorite verses in all of the Bible. In that verse Jesus says, "Behold, I stand at the door and knock. If anyone hears My voice and opens the door, I will come in to him and dine with him, and he with Me."

The problem with this translation is that it sounds too formal.

Who says behold anymore? When you knock on someone's door, you usually don't say, "BEHOLD!"

I'm not making fun of the statement of Jesus; I'm just saying that the translation doesn't relate very well. So to bring it into modern vernacular, Jesus is saying, "I'm at the door. Open up. Hey, it's your Friend out here."

Yes, that's a very loose paraphrase. But you get the idea. What is Jesus saying? He's saying, "I want to come into your life. I want to be a part of everything you're doing. Let's have a meal together. I want to spend time with you."

Personally, I don't enjoy eating with people I don't know. I keep thinking, *Maybe they're trying to sell me something.* And I just can't relax. When it comes to eating a meal, I only want to eat with someone who is a friend or family member or someone I'm comfortable with. I want to eat my food and steal some of theirs, too. That's how you know you are with a really good friend—when you can take the food off their plate without asking.

Jesus is saying, "Come on. Let's drop the pretenses. Let's get real here. I want to be your friend. I want to have fellowship with you. I want to spend time with you." He's saying, "I want to hang out with you. We'll order dessert and some coffee. I've got all the time in the world, and I'm interested in everything you have to say. I want fellowship, friendship, and intimacy with you."

That's intimacy. That is God with us.

The very thought of this should touch us deeply. Just to think that God, the almighty Creator of the universe, would be vitally interested in someone like you or me, to think that He actually wants to be a part of all we say and do—how could it be true? And yet it is true.

One of the songs that I like to sing at this time of year is the Christmas hymn, "O Come, O Come, Emmanuel":

> O come, O come, Emmanuel,
> And ransom captive Israel,
> That mourns in lonely exile here
> Until the Son of God appear.
>
> Rejoice! Rejoice! Emmanuel
> Shall come to thee, O Israel.

We sing that. But do we want that? Do we? *Do we want Immanuel to come? Do we really want Him to be a part of our lives—not just at Christmas, but all year long?* Christmas is coming, and . . . Christmas is almost over. The presents will be opened, and all that pretty paper will be in the trash can at the curb, along with the tree. You'll soon be tired of those new toys and gadgets, and you'll move on to other things.

CONCLUSION

But if you have Immanuel, what does it matter?

Christmas comes and goes, but Immanuel stays—forever.

NOTES

Chapter 2: A Twisted Family Tree

1. Susan Brink, "Suicide: holidays' darkest myth," *Los Angeles Times*, December 17, 2007, http://articles.latimes.com/2007/dec/17/health/he-xmasdepress17.

Chapter 3: Christmas, the Prequel

1. R. Kent Hughes, *The Gift of Christmas* (Wheaton, IL: Crossway, 2003), 11.

Chapter 4: What's in a Name?

1. Bertrand Russell, *The Conquest of Happiness* (Abingdon, UK: Routledge, 2006), 38.
2. Will Lester, "Americans admit: We're hooked on high-tech gadgets," *Casper Star Tribune*, December 23, 2005, http://trib.com/news/national/americans-admit-we-re-hooked-on-high-tech-gadgets/article_490df58a-5623-576a-97e2-9a48e84585ef.html.
3. Max Lucado, *God Came Near* (Nashville, TN: Thomas Nelson, 2004), 7.

Chapter 6: Don't Miss Christmas

1. Rocky A., "Wright Brothers telegram," *Flickr.com*, taken October 14, 2007, accessed July 15, 2014, https://www.flickr.com/photos/asmythie/1569550395/in/photolist-3emqVu-9eHYns-tEsAP-

63tqii-3UN759-3oGmDH-9eETxR-9eF2Se-9eESPc-jRZ6Y6-kZVyuc-abxUJZ-79zDuk-3eh24K-66Wh3n. Digital image.

2. Robert M. Kane, *Air Transportation,* 14th ed. (Dubuque, IA: Kendall Hunt, 2003), 64.

Chapter 9: The Man Who Tried to Stop Christmas

1. John F. MacArthur, *The MacArthur New Testament Commentary: Matthew 1–7* (Chicago: Moody, 1985), 46.

Chapter 11: The Promise of Christmas

1. Ray C. Stedman, *Authentic Christianity* (Grand Rapids, MI: Discovery House Publishers, 1996), Kindle edition.

2. C. S. Lewis, *Made for Heaven: And Why on Earth It Matters* (New York: HarperCollins Publishers, 2005), 19–20.

3. Henry Wadsworth Longfellow, "Christmas Bells," in *The Complete Poetical Works of Henry Wadsworth Longfellow* (Boston, 1880), 289–290.

Chapter 12: Christmas, the Main Event

1. R. Kent Hughes and Ron DiCianni, *The Gift: Seven Meditations on the Events Surrounding Jesus' Birth* (Wheaton, IL: Crossway, 1994), 38.

2. G. K. Chesterton, *The Everlasting Man* (EMP Books, 2012), 137.

3. Saint Augustine, *Sermons on the Liturgical Seasons,* trans. Mary Sarah Muldowney (Washington, DC: The Catholic University of America Press, 1959), 13.

Chapter 13: The True Gift of Christmas

1. Corrie ten Boom, *Tramp for the Lord* (Fort Washington, PA: CLC Publications, 2011), 55.

2. Charles R. Swindoll, *The Mystery of God's Will* (Nashville, TN: Thomas Nelson, 1999), 165.

3. Robert Andrews, *The Columbia Dictionary of Quotations*, s. v. "possessions" (New York: Columbia University Press, 1993), 715.

ABOUT THE AUTHOR

Greg Laurie is the senior pastor of Harvest Christian Fellowship in Riverside and Orange County in California. Harvest is one of the largest churches in the United States and consistently ranks among the most influential churches in the country. He recently celebrated forty years as the senior pastor. In 1990, he began holding large-scale public evangelistic events called Harvest Crusades. More than five million people have attended Harvest events around the world, and more than 421,800 people have registered professions of faith through these outreaches.

He is the featured speaker of the nationally syndicated radio program *A New Beginning,* which is broadcast on more than seven hundred radio outlets worldwide. Along with his work at Harvest Ministries, he served as the 2013 honorary chairman of the National Day of Prayer and also serves on the board of directors of the Billy Graham Evangelistic Association.

He has authored over seventy books, including *As It Is in Heaven; Revelation: the Next Dimension; As I See It; Hope for Hurting Hearts; Married. Happily; Every Day with Jesus; Signs of the Times; Hope for America;* and many more.

RED

He has been married to Cathe Laurie for forty years, and they have two sons, Christopher and Jonathan. Christopher went to be with the Lord in 2008. They also have five grandchildren.

Other Books by Greg Laurie

KERYGMA
PUBLISHING

Visit: www.AllenDavidBooks.com